food from
green places

food from Green Places

vegetarian recipes from garden & hedgerow

ROSAMOND RICHARDSON

photographs by Robin Matthews

WEIDENFELD & NICOLSON
London

contents

Introduction

The concept of a 'rural idyll' is deeply ingrained in the human psyche: the Garden of Eden is mankind's original myth. The powerful longing for some connection with the countryside, with things natural, is a desire for peace, tranquillity and security away from the insanities of urban life. People find this in their own ways: if they are not able to live in the country, they may find a personal oasis through tending their own garden, of whatever size and in whatever situation, to produce food from green places.

My life was rich: I took a swarm of bees

And found a crumpled snake skin on the road,

All in one day, and was increased by these.

I have not understood humanity.

But those plain things, that gospel of each year,

Made me the scholar of simplicity.

The Land, Vita Sackville-West, 1926

Here the echoes of a rural past still ring clear. For centuries our predecessors have harvested their garden produce through the turning seasons of the year. They have gathered food from field and hedgerow, tended their fruit trees and bushes, worked on the vegetable plot, and planted herb gardens for medicinal as well as culinary use. The more dedicated have kept bees and produced their own honey for themselves and their neighbours. Many have had chickens scratching around to produce free-range eggs, and the more courageous naturalists have foraged for mushrooms in spring and autumn. Country folk have made wines, cordials and herbal teas for generations, using all manner of basic materials: their skill was in making use of everything that grew around them as well as what they cultivated, and in knowing their various properties and qualities.

It is a long heritage, starting locally in the West with the monastic gardens of the Middle Ages, but basically stretching back to the ancient history of the Far East, Egypt, the Middle East and ancient Greece and Rome. The botanical names of fruits, flowers, herbs and vegetables reflect their far-flung origins and cultures, and their history is full of fascinating stories. The gardens of the East are now but legend, but we can still find traces of the earliest Western infirmary gardens planted by medieval monks. From there it is a rich trail through sixteenth-century formal gardens to the great age of the stately home in the eighteenth and early nineteenth centuries, until we reach the softer influence of Gertrude Jekyll and William Robinson as they returned full circle to the more natural look of the cottage garden. Yet whatever the scale of the garden and however humble or elegant its design, the underlying purpose has always been twofold: the harvesting of home-grown produce and the joy of living with plants in the garden.

The garden harvest tells us much about economic history at any given moment in time. Food is a social barometer; it is closely connected with the fluctuations of civilization. It is also about self-sufficiency, about making use of everything that we can grow, and of the plants in the wild. In addition, the many myths attached to these plants have been woven into a rich tapestry of folklore over the centuries, which is just as alive today as it ever was. Delving into old recipe books takes us directly into the insights of our forebears, and many an old manuscript provides amusing comments or instructions which capture the feeling of a particular time.

They describe old country traditions, many of which are still extant today in parts of rural Europe.

The style of cooking in *Food From Green Places* owes much to this rural heritage. Some of it is traditional English country cooking, some of it owes something to the more eclectic styles of modern living. But the majority of recipes have an intrinsically peasant quality to them – simplicity and honesty being the keynotes. The concession to healthy eating is evident: whereas in the past people ate a diet rich in animal fats, the recipes in this book tend to favour vegetable margarines over butter, and make plentiful use of olive and sunflower oils. The use of sugar is kept low, and *crème fraîche* and Greek yoghurt replace single and double cream. Where you are using much of your own organic produce, it is logical to use free-range eggs and foods which have minimum processing, such as unbleached sugar and wholemeal or unbleached flours, or a balance of both. The food has an integrity; it is natural and wholesome, healthy and clean. Food from green places is good food. It is also a personal response to the mysterious subtlety and awesome beauty of the seasonal cycle.

abundant *Orchards*

An apple I took of a tree

God had it forbidden me

Wherefore I should damned be

14th century ms, *Anon*

According to legend, Mesopotamia's Garden of Eden was full of fruit trees, and Middle Eastern orchards were also pleasure gardens. The word 'orchard' means enclosed garden, and would usually shelter apple, pear and plum trees. The Song of Songs sings, 'As the apple tree among the trees of the orchard, so is my beloved among the young men.'

In medieval Europe, fruit was used more for making drinks than for eating, and cider was the most common drink in England in the Middle Ages. Desserts, heavily sweetened and spiced, appear in manuscript recipes, and preserves were commonplace in all households, providing variety during the lean winter months. Cottagers and smallholders invariably had one or two fruit trees for their own use, enabling them to stock the larder. Their cottage gardens provided means of self-sufficiency: a vegetable patch, chickens, perhaps a pig, a beehive or two, and at the very least an apple tree. For the richer, as part of their larger estates, a formal orchard might be enclosed within the kitchen garden or set just outside its vine-clad walls.

Legendary from the earliest times, the apple became highly symbolic in biblical and mythological terms, being a sign of fertility and good luck. Apples probably came to England with the Romans, before which time the crab apple was widely used in drinks, vinegars and sour cooking cider. The pear became a symbol of delight, and Edward I commanded 'peares' to be planted in his garden at Westminster: the Kings of England were the principal fruit growers in their land. The wild pear, native to England, was popular in preserves, jams and puddings, and perry was a popular drink among country folk. The quince was the next favourite, used for marmalades, jellies and preserves. According to archive records, the King's gardener at the Palace of Westminster bought a lot of quince, pear and apple trees in 1292, the quinces costing 41 shillings per 100, the same price as a peach tree but vastly more expensive than a cherry tree which in those days fetched about 1s 6d (10p) per 100.

Peaches feature in medieval literature from the thirteenth century onwards, usually classed as exotic fruit,

and were a royal favourite. *The Chronicle of Roger of Wendover*, 1210, tells us that King John hastened his own death by indulging in 'a surfeit of peaches and ale'. The fruit of the curious medlar, that Chaucer called a 'homely tree', was made into preserves by many, and the gardener at Westminster Abbey was ordered to supply the community with *'apples, cherries in season, plums, big pears, nuts and mepsilia [medlars] if he has them in his garden'*. The fruit was stored in straw for a month, from October to November, when it was eaten in its softened state, either raw or puréed with honey.

Not everyone bothered to cultivate plums in those days, since wild plums were plentiful: John Gerard's *Herbal* of 1597 refers to cultivars as 'manured', and in his day the gardens at Westminster Abbey won acclaim for the sweetness of their cultivated plums. Damsons, bullace and sloes were gathered from country lanes in autumn as part of the annual wild harvest. Mulberries, eaten ripe from the tree, were also deemed useful as a food dye, and their juice, which makes an invigorating drink in its own right, was added both to wine and to plum 'pottage'.

Raspberries were picked wild rather than cultivated: they grew prolifically alongside elderberries, blackberries and bilberries in English lanes and hedgerows. Strawberries, on the other hand, were imported as early as the thirteenth century, and by the fifteenth century they had become fashionable, often sold by the street sellers of London. The earliest record of cultivated gooseberries, which even though native to Britain were rarely used in the Middle Ages, is dated 1275, in the reign of Edward I. Interestingly enough, they featured only in savoury dishes. Cherries, eaten 'wine-red', were widely cultivated and highly valued: King Henry VIII's fruiterer established cherry orchards at Newington in Kent, an area still famous for its fruit.

Over the following centuries, as the art of gardening developed, orchards and kitchen gardens evolved from purely practical considerations into the beginnings of an art form: the legacy of the medieval arbour becomes the inspiration for a tunnel of fruit trees trained over an iron frame, the traditional 'potager' evolves from monastic plots, and the beauty of espaliered fruit trees graces many a sunny wall in many a land.

Traditional APPLE TART

There are endless versions of apple pies, tarts and flans. Gervase Markham's *The English Housewife* of 1683 gives a traditional English recipe:

TO MAKE APPLE TART: Take apples and peel them, and slice them thin from the core into a pan with white wine, good store of sugar, cinnamon and rose water, and so boil all till it be thick. Then cool it and strain it, and beat it very well together with a spoon, and then put it into your crust and bake it. It carrieth the colour red.

A p p l e s

According to Genesis, the apple was the first fruit of the world's creation. Cooks through the ages have invented countless ways of using them, and here are some recipes which include a number of traditional old English ideas, adapted to modern tastes and techniques. Many have the flavour of peasant cuisine – English country cooking at its most genuine and natural.

Autumnal Apple Crisp

These fragrantly spiced apples have a unique freshness and crunchy texture, and the crisp topping of this wonderful pudding is mouthwatering. You can use pears in place of the apples, as both fruits make a memorable and original dessert.

SERVES 6

225 g (8 oz) day-old breadcrumbs

grated nutmeg and mixed spice, for dusting

700 g (1½ lb) cooking apples, peeled and cored

sugar to taste

1 teaspoon mixed spice

40 g (1½ oz) candied lemon peel, chopped

a little butter or margarine

Grease a 20 cm (8 in) pie dish and cover thickly with 50 g (2 oz) of breadcrumbs. Dust with a sprinkling of nutmeg and mixed spice.

Coarsely grate the apples and mix with 25 g (1 oz) of the breadcrumbs, sugar to taste, the 1 teaspoon mixed spice and the candied peel. Pile into the prepared dish. Cover the top thickly with the last of the breadcrumbs and dot with butter or margarine. Bake in a preheated oven at 190°C/375°F/mark 5 for 30 minutes, until the crust is crisp and brown. It is delicious hot or warm.

An old recipe book recommends serving this with hot chocolate sauce. My preference would be for thick Greek yoghurt or perhaps custard (see *Crème Anglaise* on page 153), although I have memories of my mother grating chocolate over a hot dish of grated, baked apples, and it was exquisite.

Nursery APPLES

There is an old English recipe which instructs the cook to core apples and fill the holes with brown sugar. They are then packed into a dish, water added to halfway up the fruit, and baked until the apples are fluffy and the sugar has boiled to toffee.

French Apple Tart
In the past, country people brought apples and medlars to church on All Saints Day as an offering to the souls of the departed, and such traditions still survive in parts of France today. The French have a great tradition of apple cookery, and make an apple tart that takes some beating for all its simplicity.

SERVES 6–8

1 recipe quantity Sweet Crust Pastry (see page 150)

4–5 medium apples

1 tablespoon lemon juice

2 large egg yolks

25–40 g (1–1½ oz) vanilla sugar

300 ml (½ pint) double cream

Roll out the pastry and use to line a greased 25 cm (10 in) tart tin. Bake blind (see page 152) in a preheated oven at 200°C/400°F/mark 6 for 15 minutes. Cool a little on a wire rack.

Peel, core and slice the apples, sprinkling them as you do so with lemon juice to prevent discoloration. Beat together the egg yolks with the vanilla sugar until thick and pale, then beat in the cream.

Arrange the apple slices in a circular pattern over the cooked pastry shell, pointed ends towards the centre. Pour over the cream mixture and bake in the oven at 190°C/375°F/mark 5 for 30–35 minutes, until the cream is nearly set firm but still slightly runny in the centre. Leave to cool slightly. Serve warm.

Apple Turnovers
Simply wonderful: crisp golden puff pastry, encased around an aromatic apple purée; these turnovers melt in the mouth.

MAKES 8

6 Cox or Blenheim Orange apples, peeled, cored
  and chopped

sugar to taste

a pinch of ground cinnamon

1 tablespoon chopped candied orange peel

2 teaspoons rosewater

1 teaspoon dill seeds (optional)

225 g (8 oz) shop-bought puff pastry, rolled out
  very thinly

groundnut or sunflower oil, for frying

caster sugar, for sprinkling

Cook the chopped apples with a little water until you have a thick, smooth purée. Sweeten to taste with a little sugar and add the cinnamon, candied peel, rosewater and dill seeds, if using.

Cut the pastry into 10 cm (4 in) squares. Place 2 tablespoons of the apple mixture on to each square, moisten the edges of the pastry with a little water and fold over to enclose the apple filling and form a triangle. Press the edges together well to seal. Fry the turnovers in 1 cm (½ in) deep hot oil, until puffed up and golden. Drain on absorbent kitchen paper and serve hot, sprinkled with caster sugar.

Apple Dice with Crisp Croûtons

This is inspired by a recipe from a very old English cookery book and is unusual and distinctive. The soft, translucent cooked apples make an excellent contrast to the crunchy croûtons.

SERVES 4

50 g (2 oz) granulated sugar

6 medium dessert apples, peeled and cored

50 g (2 oz) butter or margarine

3 slices day-old bread, crusts removed and cut into small cubes

1–2 tablespoons Demerara sugar

thick Greek yoghurt or *crème fraîche*, to serve

Place the sugar in a medium-sized bowl. Cut the apples into dice and add to the sugar. Toss to coat well. Melt half of the butter or margarine in a heavy frying pan, and toss the sugared apples over a medium heat, stirring, until they go a golden brown colour and the texture is sticky. Remove and put on a warm platter.

Add the rest of the butter or margarine to the pan, and more if necessary, and fry the bread cubes so that they mop up the juices and caramel from the apples. When they are crisp all over, toss over the apples and serve immediately, sprinkled with Demerara sugar. Hand round a bowl of *crème fraîche* or thick Greek yoghurt to serve.

Drying APPLES

Peel and core as many apples as required, then thinly slice crosswise to make rings. As you go, put the rings into salted water (25 g/1 oz salt per 1 litre/1¾ pints water) so that they don't discolour.

Drain and dry thoroughly on a towel. Place on wire racks and leave to dry out in a very low oven (120°C/250°F/mark ½) with the door left open, or in the airing cupboard. The time taken will vary with the water content of the fruit. When the apple rings are ready, they will become slightly leathery and barely crisp to the touch.

Then cool them thoroughly and pack into transparent paper bags – but not plastic bags, as these will encourage mould.

Alternatively, you can string the apple rings up and hang them over the boiler or Aga to dry. Move them around from time to time so that every surface has a chance to dry out completely.

To use dried apples, soak them in warm water for an hour or so to rehydrate them. Wipe dry and they are then ready to use.

Stuffed Apple Dumplings *Stuffing apples with blackberries is an inspiration, and wrapping them in a light pastry casing makes an autumn dessert to remember.*

SERVES 4

4 large cooking apples, Bramleys for preference

225 g (8 oz) blackberries, washed and hulled, or

   sultanas (or both)

2 tablespoons granulated sugar

a little butter or margarine

1½ recipe quantities Sweet Crust Pastry (see

   page 150)

beaten egg, to glaze

Crème Anglaise (see page 153), to serve

Peel and core the apples, and hollow out the centres a little to make cavities for the fruit. Roll the blackberries or sultanas (or mixture of both) in a little sugar, and pack them lightly into the cavities. Top with knobs of butter or margarine.

Roll out the pastry thinly and cut into 4 squares, each large enough to encase an apple. Put one apple into the centre of each pastry square, draw up the corners and pinch them together over the top of the fruit. Dampen and pinch the open edges together. Brush with beaten egg, and place in a greased baking dish. Bake in a preheated oven at 180°C/350°F/mark 4 for 25–30 minutes, until the pastry is golden and the apple inside soft. Serve with *Crème Anglaise*.

Apple Ratafia *There is a tradition in Brittany that the apple pickers leave one last and best apple on the end of the highest branch. If it is still there after leaf-fall, there will be a good crop in the orchard the following year. Whether the crop is light or heavy, this apple dessert is exceptionally good – different in style and delicate in flavour.*

SERVES 6

450 g (1 lb) apples, peeled, cored and chopped

100 g (4 oz) sugar

1 glass white wine

50 g (2 oz) butter or margarine

juice and grated rind of ½ lemon

4 egg yolks

50 g (2 oz) ratafias or small macaroons, crushed to

   coarse crumbs

custard or whipped cream, to serve

Stew the apples with the sugar and wine until you have a thick, smooth purée, stirring frequently. Cool a little. Mix in the butter or margarine and the lemon juice and rind, and leave until almost cold. Beat the egg yolks thoroughly, and stir them in. Fold in the crushed ratafias. Place in a greased baking dish.

Bake in a preheated oven at 180°C/350°F/mark 4 for 40 minutes until firm in the centre. Leave to stand for at least 15 minutes before serving. Serve warm, with custard or whipped cream, or cold just as it is.

Pears

There are about 5,000 named varieties of pear, a native of eastern Europe and the Middle East, of which between twenty and thirty are cultivated on a large scale.

The Williams is the emperor of its species. It is set off by fine cheese (with a special affinity for blue cheeses), and is as wonderful in a salad as in a classic fruit tart. Baking the pears in red wine has become a classic recipe (see page 17), and the liqueur *Poire Williams* is of the finest flavour and delicacy.

The pear came into its own in the seventeenth century in France, which became the main country for pear cultivation and cookery. The Comice pear, 'Doyenne du Comice', was raised in Angers, the capital of Anjou, and although the original garden has long since disappeared, Comice pears are still widely grown there.

It is best to pick or buy pears firm, then allow them to ripen in the house. When they do, store them in the fridge, since they quickly lose that perfection of texture which is evident at their peak condition. The supreme pear, the Williams, however, has to be eaten at its point of perfect ripeness. This wonderful fruit, the culmination of 2,000 years of cultivation, has a peak moment in its development, which when captured offers a memorable gastronomic experience. Some enthusiasts have been reported as getting up at three in the morning in order to seize this moment of perfection!

Pears in VINE LEAVES

A SIXTEENTH-CENTURY RECIPE: *Lay a layer of vine leaves in an earthen pot, and over them peeled and halved pears. Repeat layers until the pot be full, putting some fine sliced ginger, and a few cloves, between each layer. Fill up the pot with as much cider as the pot will hold, and lay some dish or board upon the pears that they do not swim, and cover the pot closely, and stew all night when the fire be low.*

Let the pears cool in the pot, and serve cold with cream or custard.

Eliza Acton's Pear Meringue *This pudding is extremely successful when made with Conference pears, the hard pears that cook up so well – they retain their crispness and do not go mushy. Flavour the pears with a little cinnamon or a few cloves if you like, for added interest to this simple but lovely dessert.*

SERVES 4

700 g (1½ lb) pears, cored and sliced

2 tablespoons soft brown sugar

5 egg whites

5 tablespoons caster sugar

Cut the pear slices into 2.5 cm (1 in) lengths. Put into a shallow baking dish with a little water, and sprinkle with the sugar. Cover the dish and bake in a preheated oven at 170°C/325°F/mark 3 for 15 minutes until the pears are softened. This will depend on the ripeness of the fruit. Leave to cool.

Whisk the egg whites until very stiff, then fold in the caster sugar carefully and lightly. Pile this meringue mixture on top of the pears, and bake in the bottom of a preheated oven at 170°C/325°F/mark 3 for 30 minutes. Cool for a few minutes before serving. This dish is also delicious cold.

Poires au Gratin *A simple fruit dessert for summer, when pears are at their best, this mixture of pears stewed with white wine and apricot jam, and covered with a crust of macaroon crumbs, is delightful.*

SERVES 6

900 g (2 lb) fresh ripe pears, peeled, cored and quartered

75 ml (3 fl oz) dry white wine

75 ml (3 fl oz) apricot jam, sieved

75 g (3 oz) macaroons, crushed

40 g (1½ oz) butter or margarine, cut into tiny dice

Crème Anglaise **(see page 153) or thick Greek yoghurt, to serve**

Slice the prepared pears, and arrange them overlapping in a dish. Heat the wine and sieved apricot jam together, and pour over the pears. Sprinkle the macaroon crumbs over the top, and dot with the butter or margarine. Bake at 200°C/400°F/mark 6 for 20–30 minutes, until the top is lightly browned. Serve hot, warm or cold with *Crème Anglaise* or thick Greek yoghurt.

French Pear Tart
This tart is simplicity itself to make and, I have to admit, one of my favourite desserts. The flavours emerge so pure and uncomplicated and the tart is so fresh and immediate that it is a winner every time.

SERVES 6

1 recipe quantity Sweet Crust Pastry (see page 150)

2 large pears, peeled, cored and sliced

1 egg and 1 egg yolk

40 g (1½ oz) sugar

1 tablespoon cornflour

150 ml (¼ pint) single cream

2 teaspoons vanilla essence

Roll out the pastry, and use to line a greased 22 cm (9 in) tart tin. Bake blind (see page 152) in a preheated oven at 190°C/375°F/mark 5 for 15 minutes. Cool a little on a wire rack.

Arrange the sliced pears over the cooled pastry. Beat the egg and egg yolk with the sugar until thick, then beat in the cornflour, cream and vanilla essence. Pour over the fruit in the pastry case.

Bake in the oven at 190°C/375°F/mark 5 for 30–40 minutes, or until puffed and golden and lightly set in the centre. Serve hot, warm or cold.

Pears Baked with Red Wine
Pears baked in red wine has become a cookery classic. A miraculous transformation occurs with the slow cooking of the fruit in the wine: the texture is wonderful and the flavour sublime. Serve this dish either warm or cold, plain as it is, or with thick Greek yoghurt or Crème Anglaise *(see page 153).*

SERVES 6

6 large pears, preferably Williams, peeled, cored
   and halved

rind of 1 lemon, cut into thin strips

50–75 g (2–3 oz) brown sugar

600 ml (1 pint) red wine

Place the pears, overlapping slightly, in a large shallow baking dish. Scatter the lemon rind over the top, and sprinkle with the sugar. Pour water over to nearly cover, then add enough wine to immerse the pears. Cover tightly with foil, and bake slowly at 150°C/300°F/mark 2 for about 2 hours until the pears are perfectly tender, turning them halfway through the cooking.

Quinces

The quince is a native of western Asia, and is the 'golden apple' of Greek mythology, the prize for a beauty contest, judged by Paris, between Athena, Hera and Aphrodite. The latter emerged triumphant, endowing her prize with the symbolism of love, marriage and fertility. Aphrodite is often represented with a quince in her hand, and there was a popular custom in ancient Greece that a bride should eat a quince before entering her nuptial bed. Honey from quince blossom is exceptionally aromatic.

> The medlar and the quince's globe of gold
>
> How rich and fat those yellow fruits do hang!
>
> *The Garden*, Vita Sackville-West, 1946

Quince Honey

Golden and pear-shaped, and with a unique fragrance, the quince makes a beautiful preserve, much enjoyed in medieval times and still just as wonderful today. This recipe is based on one from a twelfth-century manuscript which had been translated from the Greek for King Edgar (c. AD 950), who is said to have imported quinces and introduced them to the Britons.

MAKES 700 G (1½ LB)

300 ml (½ pint) honey

100 ml (3½ fl oz) water

450 g (1 lb) quinces

a small piece of root ginger, peeled and finely grated (optional)

Place the honey and water into a saucepan and cook over a medium heat until you have a fairly thick syrup. Chop the quinces small and boil them in the honey syrup until soft, about 45 minutes. Rub through a sieve. Return to the pan and bring to the boil again, then simmer fast until the mixture reaches 100°C/200°F and forms a clear, dark rose-coloured honey. Add a little finely grated ginger to flavour, if desired, and leave to cool. Pot, seal and store in a dark, cool place. Use as a flavoured, thick honey on fresh bread or muffins, and enjoy its old-fashioned and truly original quality.

Right: *Quince honey*

Quince Cream
During the sixteenth and seventeenth centuries hundreds of recipes for quinces appeared in cookery books, and this is an adaptation of one of them. It is a beautiful and unusual cream, a stunning rose-pink colour, and makes a lovely autumn dessert.

SERVES 6

450 g (1 lb) quinces

caster sugar to taste

25 g (1 oz) candied peel, chopped

50 g (2 oz) glacé cherries, sliced

250 ml (8 fl oz) *crème fraîche*

Cut up the quinces, place in a saucepan with enough water to cover and bring to the boil. Lower the heat, cover and simmer for about 40 minutes until they turn to a pink mush. Leave to cool for several hours or overnight (the seeds give out a lot of 'jelly').

Rub the pulp through a sieve and sweeten to taste with sugar. Fold in the candied peel, glacé cherries and *crème fraîche*. Pour into a mould and chill for 5–6 hours or overnight.

To serve, spoon into dessert bowls.

Cotignac
Cotignac has a taste and texture which for me conjure up my childhood. We had an old quince tree in the garden, and when there was a good crop my mother used to make this delectable preserve. It is served in thick, rich slices, and is mouthwatering with coeur à la crème *or light cream cheese for an unusual dessert.*

MAKES 2.7 KG (6 LB)

2 kg (4 lb) quinces

300 ml (½ pint) water

sugar

Cut up the quinces. Put them into a heavy pan with the water. Bring to the boil, and simmer until the fruit is tender. When very soft, mash with a potato masher, then push through a sieve. Weigh the purée, and put it back into the pan with an equal weight of sugar. Stir over a gentle heat until the sugar dissolves, then turn the heat up and boil until the mixture thickens and turns dark red. Keep a sharp eye on it, and stir constantly to avoid burning.

When the purée is really thick, remove the pan from the heat, and pot in warm jars, packing it down well. Cover and seal (see page 145), and store in a cool, dark place. To serve, scoop it out and slice into rounds.

Rhubarb Rhubarb's country of origin is Siberia (the old name for Russia is 'Rus', hence its name). It found its way east and became, with its purgative qualities, one of the primary plants used in Chinese medicine. Rhubarb was introduced from Russia to Britain in 1578, and is the first fruit of our spring, its tender young pink stems making succulent fillings for pies and crumbles, and an excellent jam. Its flavour mingles exceptionally well with elderflower, ginger, orange and also angelica.

Rhubarb Oat Crunch *This makes a perfect finale to a family meal. The crunchy, crumbly oat topping is mouthwatering. Pick the tender, young stalks of the rhubarb for this recipe, rather than older, tougher ones, as their delicate pink does much to enhance the enjoyment of this dish.*

SERVES 6

450 g (1 lb) rhubarb, trimmed and cut into
   5 cm (2 in) lengths

granulated sugar to taste

100 g (4 oz) Demerara sugar

50 g (2 oz) margarine

50 g (2 oz) oats

25 g (1 oz) plain flour

2 tablespoons sunflower seeds

thick Greek yoghurt or *Crème Anglaise* (see page
   153), to serve

Put the rhubarb into an ovenproof dish with a little water, and cover it. Bake in a preheated oven at 170°C/325°F/mark 3 for 20–30 minutes, until tender. Alternatively you can microwave it. Add granulated sugar to taste. Cool and drain.

Cream the Demerara sugar with the margarine, and mash in the oats. Sift in the flour, and mix well until crumbly. Finally mix in the sunflower seeds.

Spread the topping over the rhubarb in a heatproof dish. Bake in the oven for 30 minutes at 180°C/350°F/mark 4 until the topping is lightly browned. Serve with thick Greek yoghurt or *Crème Anglaise*.

Plums Plums and greengages, damsons and medlars add to the abundance of autumn's annual harvest from the orchard.

All Plums are under Venus, and are like women, somebetter and some worse. As there is a great diversity of kinds, so there is in the operation of Plums, for some that are sweet moisten the stomach, and make the belly soluble: those that are sour quench thirst more, and bind the belly. The moist and waterish do sooner corrupt in the stomach, but the firm do nourish more, and offend less.

Herbal, Nicholas Culpeper, 1653

Plum Pie *A classic of English country cooking, this fruit pie is entirely enclosed in pastry and filled with cinnamon-scented plums and a few chopped walnuts. Use 'wet' walnuts if you can, fresh off the tree – since plums and walnuts are in season at the same time. You can also make this pie with greengages and almonds.*

SERVES 4–6

¾ recipe quantity Shortcrust Pastry (see page 150)

450 g (1 lb) plums, washed, halved, stoned and chopped

100 g (4 oz) Demerara sugar

50 g (2 oz) walnuts, chopped

2 teaspoons ground cinnamon

grated rind of ½ lemon

grated rind of ½ orange

15 g (½ oz) butter or margarine, cut into small cubes

beaten egg, to glaze

thick Greek yoghurt or custard, to serve

Roll out two-thirds of the pastry, and use to line a 20 cm (8 in) greased pie dish. Mix the prepared plums with the sugar, walnuts, cinnamon and grated rinds, and put into the pastry shell. Dot with the butter or margarine. Roll out the remaining pastry, and use to cover the pie.

Moisten the edges, and press them well together with a fork. With a sharp knife, slice a little hole in the top of the pie. Brush with beaten egg to glaze. Bake in a preheated oven at 190°C/375°F/mark 5 for 45–50 minutes. Serve warm, with thick Greek yoghurt or custard.

Jalousie
When plums hang heavy on the branch, or lie red and gold in the long grass, this melting piece of pâtisserie is definitely one of autumn's delights. Serve it with a cup of coffee at any time of the day, or as a delicious dessert served with ice cream.

SERVES 4

175 g (6 oz) puff pastry

225 g (8 oz) plums, washed, halved and stoned

sugar to taste

ground cinnamon to taste

40 g (1½ oz) walnuts, chopped (optional)

1 egg yolk, beaten

Roll out the pastry, and cut it into two oblongs. Put one on a greased baking sheet, and brush around the rim with water. Slice the plums, and arrange the slices over the surface of the pastry, leaving a margin. Sprinkle with sugar and cinnamon to taste and the chopped walnuts, if using.

Fold the other oblong of pastry in half lengthwise, and cut a series of parallel lines across the middle, leaving a margin. Open out, and lay over the plum slices. Press the edges of the pastry together well. Brush with the beaten egg yolk, and bake in a preheated oven at 220°C/425°F/mark 7 for 15 minutes. Lower the heat to 180°C/350°F/mark 4, and cook for a further 10 minutes, until well risen and golden and the plums are tender. Cool on a wire rack.

Iced Plum Soufflé
An elegant pièce de resistance, *this lightly frozen, fruit meringue is served ice cold, but still soft enough to spoon easily out of the dish. The sharp taste of ripe plums is an excellent foil to the creaminess of this memorable dessert.*

SERVES 4–6

450 g (1 lb) Victoria plums, peeled, stoned and
  chopped

1 tablespoon lemon juice

4 tablespoons eau-de-vie or Mirabelle (optional)

175 g (6 oz) sugar

125 ml (4 fl oz) water

4 egg whites

300 ml (½ pint) double cream, whipped, or
  crème fraîche

Place the chopped plums with the lemon juice and a little added water in a saucepan. Cover, and cook over a medium heat until soft. Drain, then purée in a blender or food processor. Check the taste, add more lemon juice if necessary. Stir in the eau-de-vie or Mirabelle, if using.

Dissolve the sugar in the water over a low heat. Bring to the boil, and boil until the syrup reaches 110°C/225°F, or a little poured on to a cold saucer starts to set.

Beat the egg whites until very stiff peaks form. Pour on the syrup straight from the heat, and continue whisking until the meringue swells into a white cloud.

Fold the whipped cream or *crème fraîche* into the meringue mixture, then fold in the plum purée. Turn into a 1.2 litre (2 pint) soufflé dish, and leave in the freezer until ready to serve. Serve icy cold, but soft enough to spoon out.

Damson Cheese *Little crooked trees, often mossy, growing along banks and in our hedgerows, yield a deep purple, wild plum in early autumn. Its name, damson, means the 'plum from Damascus', short for the romantic Damascene. Country people made 'cheeses' from many wild fruits, and some old damson cheeses are known to have been made a foot high and a foot across, although the average was jam-jar size. Turned out on to a plate, they were sliced, stuck with split almonds, and served with port poured over them.*

YOU WILL NEED: • **damsons, washed** • **sugar**

Put the damsons into a baking dish with a little water, and cook in a preheated oven at 170°C/325°F/mark 3 for about 30 minutes, until the juices run freely and the stones are loose. Remove and reserve the stones. Put the fruit through a sieve, or purée in a blender or food processor.

Crack open the stones, and remove the kernels. Add them to the fruit pulp, and weigh it. Place in a clean stainless steel pan, and to every 450 g (1 lb), add 450 g (1 lb) sugar. Place over a gentle heat, and simmer until a little gels when placed on a saucer (see page 145). Put the 'cheese' into straight-sided jars, and cover them closely. Seal, and store in a cool, dark place.

Leave for at least six months; it improves with keeping up to 2 years. At its best it will have shrunk a little from the sides of the jar, and the top will be crusted with sugar.

Baked DAMSONS

This simple way of cooking damsons retains all their flavour and colour, and it is a wonderful autumn dessert.

Pack your damsons into a heatproof dish, cover with sugar, and fill with water to the level of the damsons. Cover closely, and bake in a preheated oven 180°C/350°F/mark 4 until the fruit is soft – about 20 minutes depending on the ripeness of the fruit. Leave covered until cold to preserve the flavour and serve chilled with *Crème Anglaise* (see page 153).

Very Good Damson Jam
This is an excellent hedgerow jam, with all the added pleasure that gathering food from the wild affords. It is delicious on the first crumpets of the autumn, eaten sitting by the fire as the evenings draw in.

YOU WILL NEED: • **ripe damsons, freshly gathered and washed** • **water** • **sugar**

Cut the damsons open, and remove the stones. Put them into a saucepan with the water to just cover, and simmer for 40 minutes. Weigh, return to the pan, and stir in half their weight in sugar. Stir over a medium heat until the sugar dissolves, and then boil for about 15 minutes, stirring and removing any scum, until the setting point is reached (see page 145). Pot, cover and seal (see page 145). Store in a cool, dark place.

If you want a very fine jam, sieve the fruit before you weigh it.

Greengage and Almond Tart
Greengages have a royal provenance: Claude, queen to François I of France in the early sixteenth century, gave her name to a tree imported from Italy, and she grew it in quantity near her palace at Blois. In the eighteenth century, Sir William Gage brought the 'prune de la reine Claude' back from France to England, lost the labels, and called it the 'green Gage's plum'. It has a delicacy all of its own, a special fruit which makes a superb tart with ground almonds and an apricot glaze.

SERVES 6–8

1 recipe quantity Sweet Crust Pastry (see page 150)

100 g (4 oz) ground almonds

225 g (8 oz) sugar

50 g (2 oz) butter or margarine, melted

1 egg yolk

4 tablespoons thick cream

1 tablespoon kirsch (optional)

900 g (2 lb) greengages, washed, halved and stoned

150 ml (¼ pint) water

3 tablespoons apricot jam

Roll out the pastry, and use to line a greased 25 cm (10 in) tart tin. Bake blind (see page 152) in a preheated oven at 190°C/375°F/mark 5 for 15 minutes, until golden and set.

Mix the ground almonds and half the sugar with the melted butter or margarine. Beat in the egg yolk and finally the cream, and kirsch if desired. Spread this mixture over the pastry base.

Poach the greengages lightly with the remaining sugar and the water. When soft, drain, reserving a little of the cooking liquid. Place the greengages carefully over the top of the cream.

Heat the apricot jam with the reserved cooking liquid, and brush the top of the fruit with this glaze. Leave to set in a cool place.

Greengage (or Plum) Chutney *Whether you use greengages or plums, this chutney makes a wonderful addition to the winter table, and is especially delicious with fresh bread and cheese for a simple lunch.*

MAKES 2 KG (4 LB)

900 g (2 lb) greengages or ripe plums, washed, halved and stoned

225 g (8 oz) apples, cored and sliced

225 g (8 oz) onions, peeled and sliced

100 g (4 oz) raisins

100 g (4 oz) carrots, peeled or scrubbed and grated

225 g (8 oz) Demerara sugar

1 tablespoon salt

1 teaspoon each ground cloves, ginger and allspice

1 small dried red chilli (optional)

600 ml (1 pint) white wine vinegar

Mix the fruits, onions, raisins, grated carrot and sugar together in a bowl. Put the salt, spices and chilli, if using, into a preserving pan, and pour in the vinegar. Bring slowly to the boil, and then add the fruit mixture. Stir well, bring to the boil again, and simmer steadily, stirring, until the chutney is thick and no pools of liquid remain on the surface. Pot, making sure that no air bubbles are trapped in the jar. Cover with plastic screw-top lids (see page 145).

Store in a cool, dark, dry place for at least 3 months before using but, as with all chutneys, they are best left for at least a year before eating.

MEDLARS

The medlar looks like a large, rounded rosehip the colour of a russet apple, and on the tree it is as hard as a brick. Medlars soften on storing; the *Child's Guide* of 1850 says: 'They are kept in moist bran for a fortnight before being rotten enough to eat.' In rich households, medlars were kept in a silver dish of moist sawdust on the sideboard.

Gather the medlars in early autumn. Spread out the hard fruit in a single layer in an airy place and keep for some weeks until they have gone soft, or 'bletted'. Eat them for dessert as they are, or scoop out the soft insides with a spoon and mix the sweet flesh with a dash of lemon juice or with cream and sugar. Serve in tiny bowls.

TO ROAST MEDLARS: Arrange softened medlars in a shallow dish, dot with butter, and scatter over a few whole cloves. Bake in a preheated oven at 190°C/375°F/mark 5 for 10 minutes. Serve as you would baked apples, with thick Greek yoghurt or custard.

Peaches
The Romans believed that the peach came from Persia, hence its botanical name *Prunus persica*. In fact, it was originally cultivated in China, where peach blossom symbolizes long life, and came to Europe by way of Persia.

Peaches were often grown in Victorian hothouses, trained up against south-facing walls. For dessert, they might be made into a salad: a glass bowl was rinsed round with a little brandy, the fruit sliced into it and barely covered with champagne and crushed white sugar candy.

Nectarines are more or less interchangeable with peaches, being a plum-skinned, smooth variety of peach. To skin either of them, pour boiling water over them in a bowl, and leave for a few minutes. Then slit the skin with a sharp knife and it will peel off easily.

Pêches Aurore
This is food for the gods: ripe peaches, and a scoop of fresh strawberry ice cream are covered with a layer of thick zabaglione – which tastes like nectar!

SERVES 2

2 large ripe peaches

100 g (4 oz) granulated sugar

300 ml (½ pint) water

1 teaspoon vanilla essence

2–3 scoops strawberry ice cream, softened slightly

ratafia biscuits, to serve

Zabaglione:

2–3 egg yolks

50 g (2 oz) caster sugar

100 ml (3½ fl oz) Marsala or sweet white wine

Skin (see above), halve and stone the peaches. Make a light syrup by boiling together the sugar and water for a few minutes. Add the vanilla essence to the syrup, then gently poach the peach halves in it for several minutes until tender.

Now prepare the zabaglione. Beat the egg yolks with the sugar in a small bowl until pale, then beat in the wine. Set over a pan of barely simmering water. Whisk steadily with a beater until the mixture bulks up and turns pale, about 5–6 minutes. Be very careful not to overheat otherwise it will curdle, then remove from the pan and whisk until cold.

Place a layer of strawberry ice cream in each individual glass dish, and place the peach halves on top. Coat with the zabaglione, and serve at once with ratafia biscuits.

Classic Peach Tart
A great favourite, this simple tart is made of shortcrust pastry, sprinkled thickly with ratafia crumbs, topped with the fruit and baked. An apricot glaze is the finishing touch. It is brilliant. This tart freezes well.

SERVES 6

1 recipe quantity Shortcrust Pastry (see page 150)

100 g (4 oz) ratafia biscuits, crushed

4–5 ripe peaches, halved, stoned and sliced

150 ml (¼ pint) water

3 tablespoons apricot jam

Roll out the pastry, and use to line a greased 22 cm (9 in) tart tin.

Sprinkle in the ratafia biscuit crumbs. Arrange the slices of peach in the pastry case in close concentric circles, starting from the outside. Bake in a preheated oven at 220°C/425°F/mark 7 for 20–25 minutes, until the pastry is lightly browned and the fruit softened. Cover with foil after 15 minutes if the tart begins to brown too deeply.

Heat the water and apricot jam together, and while the tart is still warm brush it with this glaze. Leave to cool, and serve warm or cold.

Stuffed Peaches
The simplicity of crushed macaroon crumbs stuffed inside the stone cavity of a ripe peach makes a fresh, light dessert. It is lovely served with very cold Zabaglione (see page 28) or Crème Anglaise *(see page 153).*

SERVES 6–8

6 large peaches, halved and stoned

150 g (5 oz) macaroons or ratafias, crushed

1 large egg yolk, beaten

1 tablespoon caster sugar

Scoop out a little more around the stone cavity of each peach half to make it larger. Mash the scooped-out peach flesh, and mix it with the macaroon or ratafia crumbs, egg yolk and sugar. Pile this mixture back into the stone cavity of each peach half, making a mound.

Place the stuffed peach halves in a lightly greased, ovenproof dish, and bake in a preheated oven at 170°C/325°F/mark 3 for 40 minutes. Allow to cool slightly before serving – a perfect dessert for a summer party, served with a sweet wine such as Beaumes de Venise.

Spiced PEACHES

You can make this wonderful preserve by following the recipe for Spiced Apricots on page 30, substituting the fruit.

Apricots

The apricot is a native of China, and has been cultivated there for over 4,000 years. It also grows abundantly in the Middle East, in Armenia and around the Black Sea. The apricot gets its name from the Latin *praecox*, meaning early, because it blossoms early in the year – after the almond and before the peach. It is therefore prone to frost, which is why it does not do well in northerly zones. This luscious, golden fruit was first brought to England from Italy in 1542 by Henry VIII's gardener, a French priest and plant expert named Jean Le Loup.

Spiced Apricots

I have been making these preserved apricots for many years, and they are one of the most outstandingly successful of the range of preserves on my larder shelf. Wonderful with a ploughman's lunch, or on a mixed buffet table, or with a simple salad meal of any kind, they are also delicious with roast chicken whether hot or cold – a versatile and popular stand-by all year round.

MAKES 2.5–2.7 KG (5–6 LB)

12 whole cloves

2 x 7.5 cm (3 in) cinnamon sticks

8 allspice berries

600 ml (1 pint) white distilled vinegar

1 kg (2¼ lb) sugar

1.5 kg (3 lb) dried apricots, or 2 kg (4 lb) fresh
  apricots, halved and stoned

Tie all the spices in a muslin bag, and bring to the boil in the vinegar. Add the sugar, and dissolve over a low heat. Add the apricots, and simmer very gently for 5–8 minutes if using fresh, 10–12 minutes if using dried. Then lift the fruit out with a slotted spoon, and pack into warm, clean jars. Boil the liquid down hard until it makes a thick syrup, pour over the apricots in the jars, then cover and seal.

Apricot TART

You can make a classic apricot tart in the same way as the French Pear Tart on page 17, substituting ripe apricots, halved and stoned, for pear slices.

Right: *Spiced apricots*

Apricot FOOL

The fruit fool is an English invention, and there are many variations on the theme. Basically, the food is a fruit purée with either cream or custard added, which is spooned into glasses and served chilled. Roughly speaking, the ratio of purée to cream or custard is half and half – you will find your own preference. Sweeten your purée according to taste, and if you wish you can add a little sugar to enhance its flavour. Fruit fools are also successfully made replacing the cream or custard with thick Greek yoghurt.

TO MAKE PURÉE: Halve and stone the apricots if fresh, choosing very ripe ones only. Purée in a blender or food processor with a little orange juice. If using dried apricots, soak them for several hours or overnight, and then purée them with a little of their soaking liquid. Fold the purée into your cream, custard or thick yoghurt, spoon into glasses and serve well chilled.

See also Gooseberry Fool on page 47.

Hunza Jam *Hunzas, the little, round, pale apricots that we can buy dried and which are so delectable just as they are, come from the Hunza valley in the Himalayas. If you have the patience, crack the stones open, and add the nutty kernels to the jam at the end of the cooking; it will be worth the trouble! This is a sublime jam.*

MAKES 700 G (1½ LB):

325 g (12 oz) dried hunza apricots

325 g (12 oz) sugar

Soak the hunzas in water to cover until quite soft. Cook them in their soaking water until pulpy, about 10–15 minutes, then cool and remove the stones. Crack the stones open with a pestle, and remove and retain the nutty kernels.

Return the hunzas to the pan, stir in the sugar and cook over a low heat until the sugar dissolves. Then boil gently to setting point (see page 145), adding the reserved hunza kernels for the last couple of minutes of cooking. Leave to stand for a little, then pot in warm, clean jars. Cover and seal (see page 145). Store in a cool, dark place.

Apricot and Almond Crumble
This is a wonderful crumble for summer, excellent family food with a hint of luxury and a touch of the exotic. Out of season, I use dried, unsulphured apricots, which are by far the best in flavour; they are mouthwatering in this recipe.

SERVES 4–6

18–20 large ripe apricots, halved and stoned

sugar to taste

50 g (2 oz) blanched slivered almonds

thick Greek yoghurt or *Crème Anglaise* (see page 153), to serve

Crumble Topping:

100 g (4 oz) plain flour

100 g (4 oz) caster sugar

75 g (3 oz) ground almonds

100 g (4 oz) butter or margarine

a few drops almond essence

Cut the apricots into quarters. Arrange the apricot quarters in a large, shallow baking dish, and sprinkle with sugar to taste.

To make the crumble topping, mix the flour, sugar and ground almonds together, then rub in the butter or margarine until crumbly. Mix in the almond essence. Spread over the fruit, and sprinkle with the slivered almonds.

Bake in a preheated oven at 200°C/400°F/mark 6 for about 35 minutes, until nicely browned. If the almonds begin to brown too much, turn the heat down to 180°C/350°F/ mark 4. Serve hot or warm, with thick Greek yoghurt or *Crème Anglaise*.

Eighteenth-Century APRICOT ICE CREAM

An inimitable ice cream is easily made following this old recipe (although obviously our freezing techniques are somewhat different!).

TO MAKE ICE CREAM: *Peel, stone and scald twelve apricots, beat them in a fine mortar, and put to them six ounces of sugar and a pint of scalding cream. Work it through a fine sieve, put it into a tin that hath a close cover, and set it in a tub of ice broken small and a large quantity of salt put among it. When you see your cream grow thick around the edges, stir it and set it in again until it is all frozen up. Then put on the lid and have ready another tub with ice and salt as before: put your tin in the middle and lay ice over and under it: let it stand four or five hours, and then dip your tin in warm water before you turn it out. You may use any sort of fruit if you have not apricots, only observe to work it fine.*

The Experienced English Housekeeper, Elizabeth Raffald, 1769

Apricot Shortcake
Apricots, although the blossoms are prone to late frosts, have been grown in England since the reign of King Henry VIII when they were imported from Italy. One of early summer's most delectable treats, this scrumptious pudding, for all its simplicity, is extremely moreish, and there are never any leftovers!

SERVES 3–4

325 g (12 oz) fresh ripe apricots, halved and stoned

2 tablespoons caster sugar

100 g (4 oz) plain flour

½ teaspoon baking powder

40 g (1½ oz) butter or margarine

75 g (3 oz) soft brown sugar

vanilla ice cream or *Crème Anglaise* (see page 153), to serve

Put the apricots into a baking dish or cake tin, and sprinkle with the caster sugar.

Sift the flour with the baking powder, and rub in the butter or margarine until the mixture is crumbly. Stir in the brown sugar, and mix well. Press the mixture down on top of the fruit with a fork.

Bake in a preheated oven at 180°C/350°F/mark 4 for 25–30 minutes, until the top is pale golden. Serve hot, warm or cold – whichever way, it is quite irresistible – with vanilla ice cream or *Crème Anglaise*.

Apricot Bavaroise
This classic French dessert shows up apricots at their very best, as one of our finest fruits. This is a dinner-party piece. Use well-ripened apricots, neither too hard nor too mushy. They should be just firm to the touch with a strong golden colour – these are the sweetest.

SERVES 4–6

325 g (12 oz) ripe apricots, halved and stoned

½ teaspoon agar-agar

6 tablespoons water

300 ml (½ pint) whipping cream or *crème fraîche*

1 tablespoon icing sugar

a little lemon juice (optional)

a few shelled pistachio nuts, to decorate

Purée the apricots in a blender or food processor. Combine the agar-agar and water in a small pan and bring to the boil, then add to the apricots in the blender, and process again to mix in. Beat the cream or *crème fraîche* with the icing sugar, and when it is stiff fold the apricot purée into it. Taste, and add more sugar and a little lemon juice if required. Pour into a lightly oiled, decorative mould. Chill in the refrigerator, preferably overnight, until set.

Turn out, and scatter a few pistachio nuts over the top and around the edge just before serving.

Figs

Figs are thought to have originated in western Asia. The fig tree is native to subtropical and warm zones although it has naturalized as far north as the British Isles. Archaeologists have shown that the Romans brought figs with them to Britain, where they have been enjoyed ever since for their luscious sweetness, and also used for their laxative properties. 'Syrup of Figs' retains a place in the *British Pharmaceutical Codex* for its laxative properties.

> Do men gather grapes of thorns, or figs of thistles?
>
> St Matthew's Gospel **7:16**

Fig Jam

If you are fortunate enough to have a fig tree that bears ripe figs, why bother to cook them? I always wonder. They are exquisite just as they are; nothing can improve on them except possibly the indulgence of thick cream. But if you ever have more than you can eat, and they are dropping off the tree, make this jam. It is a masterpiece, and both breakfast and tea time are transformed by it.

MAKES 2 KG (4 LB)

1.5 kg (3 lb) figs

700 g (1½ lb) sugar

juice and grated rind of 2 lemons

Wipe the figs clean, remove the stems, and then chop them roughly. Put into the top part of a double-boiler and cover with the sugar. Add a little water to moisten. Cover with a lid, and cook over boiling water for 30–40 minutes, until the sugar has dissolved and the fruit is quite soft.

Transfer the mixture to a preserving pan, and add the lemon rind and juice, stirring well. Bring to the boil, and boil rapidly for about 8–10 minutes, stirring, until the jam thickens and reaches the setting point (see page 145). Pot in warm clean jars, cover and seal (see page 145). Store in a cool, dark place.

Strawberries A beautiful and kind young girl, according to

the Brothers Grimm, was driven out by her stepmother to find strawberries in the snow. Lost in

the forest, she came across a dwarves' house, and shared her crust of bread with them. They

offered her shelter, and as she swept the snow aside from the doorway with their broom, she

found strawberries growing.

The image of the red fruit in the snow in the dark forest is a compelling one. The strawberry,

a member of the rose family, has a particular attraction: its colour is wonderful, and it is unique

among fruits in having the seeds dotted around on the outside rather than embedded within.

Strawberry Shortcake *Strawberry shortcake is one of summer's great treats, with its*
layers of crumbly biscuit, whipped cream and juicy strawberries. A wonderful dessert for a meal alfresco, lingering over
its flavours in the sunshine.

SERVES 6

325 g (12 oz) flour, half wholemeal and half plain

1 teaspoon baking powder

225 g (8 oz) butter or margarine

175 g (6 oz) light brown sugar

700 g (1½ lb) strawberries, washed and hulled

caster sugar

450 ml (¾ pint) double cream, whipped

Sift the flour with the baking powder, and rub in the butter or margarine until the mixture resembles fine
breadcrumbs. Mix in the sugar. Press the mixture into two 20 cm (8 in) buttered sandwich tins, and bake in a
preheated oven at 170°C/325°F/mark 3 for 30–40 minutes, until a light golden colour. Cool in the tins before
turning out.

Slice the strawberries, reserving a few whole ones for decoration, and toss the slices in caster sugar. Place
half of them on top of one of the shortcake rounds, and cover with a thick layer of whipped cream. Top with
the other round of shortcake. Cover the top with another layer of slices strawberries, then a layer of whipped
cream, and decorate with the reserved whole strawberries. Keep in a cool place until ready to serve.

Strawberries in Cream
This is a superb way to serve strawberries, but it comes with a warning: 'Raw cream, eaten with strawberries, is a rural man's banquet: yet I have known such banquets hath put men in jeopardy of their lives, by the excess thereof.'

Dietary of Health, Andrew Boorde, 1547

SERVES 4

450 ml (¾ pint) double cream or *crème fraîche*

700 g (1½ lb) strawberries, washed and hulled

icing sugar, to dust

Whip the cream or *crème fraîche* lightly. Cut the larger strawberries in half, leaving the small ones whole. Drop into the cream, stirring and mashing lightly until the cream won't hold any more fruit. It will be a wonderful pale pink colour. Sprinkle with a dusting of icing sugar and 'serve forth, in June, on a green lawn, under shady trees by the river'.

This also works beautifully as a filling for a light sponge.

Strawberry Jam
At the height of the strawberry season each year, I make this very simple jam, which never lasts long because it is so popular. It is unbeatable on freshly made scones for a summery tea in the garden, and also makes an excellent filling for sponge cake.

MAKES 2.5 KG (5 LB)

1.5 kg (3 lb) strawberries, washed and hulled

1 kg (2¼ lb) preserving sugar

2 thick slices of lemon

Put all the ingredients into a preserving pan with a little water, and simply boil to setting point (see page 145). Remove the slices of lemon, and put the jam into warm, clean jars. Cover and seal (see page 145), and store in a dark, cool place.

Strawberry SAUCE

You can make the simplest of strawberry sauces to go with ice cream, or with fresh peaches, for example. It freezes well, and is one of the best ways of saving these berries for the winter months. Simply purée washed, hulled strawberries with a little caster sugar to taste in a blender or food processor until smooth. Strain through a sieve to remove the pips, and add a little orangeflower water if you wish for an exotic touch.

A *tart of* STRAWBERRIES

Pick and wash your Strawberries clean, and put them in the pastry one by another, as thick as you can. Then take Sugar, Cinnamon and a little Ginger finely beaten, and well mingled together, and cast them on the strawberries. Cover them with the lid finely cut into Lozenges, and so let them bake a quarter of an hour.

A Book of Fruits and Flowers, Thomas Jenner, 1653

English Summer Pudding *The most English of recipes, summer pudding is one of high summer's peak culinary experiences, though on the face of it this appears rather unlikely because of its seeming banality. Old English recipes made frequent use of bread, usually resulting in rather heavy dishes, but this is quite wonderful, and is a masterpiece of English country cooking.*

SERVES 6

325 g (12 oz) strawberries, washed, hulled and
   halved

225 g (8 oz) raspberries, washed and hulled

225 g (8 oz) blackcurrants or redcurrants, washed,
   topped and tailed

100 g (4 oz) cherries, halved and stoned

5 tablespoons water

75 g (3 oz) sugar

10–12 slices wholemeal bread

Crème Anglaise (see page 153) or thick Greek
   yoghurt, to accompany

Place all the prepared fruits in a large pan with the water. Stir over a gentle heat until well mixed, then simmer gently for about 5 minutes. Stir in the sugar, remove from the heat and leave to cool.

Butter an 18 cm (7 in) cake tin or 900 ml (1½ pint) pudding basin. Trim the crusts from the bread. Cut some of the slices in half lengthwise, and use to line the sides of the tin or basin. Cut more of the slices into triangles, and use to line the bottom of the tin or basin, making sure that the edges fit neatly together. Fill with the fruit and enough of the juice to moisten the bread, including around the sides. Cover the top with more bread triangles, and pour over more juice, making sure that every bit of bread is moistened.

Place a flat plate over the pudding to weight it down, and leave overnight. To serve, invert it on to a serving dish, and pass *Crème Anglaise* or thick Greek yoghurt around to go with it.

Raspberries Raspberries have grown wild all over Britain

for centuries, and it is considered opinion that Scottish raspberries are the best in the world for

flavour. They like damp, and a brisk climate, which Perthshire, where the best raspberries are

grown commercially, provides for them. Some gardeners claim that yellow raspberries have a

superior flavour, mild and sweet, but whatever the colour many think that the best way to eat

them is fresh off the vine with thick cream and sugar. Back in the seventeenth century, garden-

lover and botanist John Parkinson called this an 'afternoon dish' in summertime; and so it still

is. Raspberries freeze quite well whole, but to my mind the best way to store them for the win-

ter is in the form of a purée, sieved and sweetened to taste – a delicious sauce with ice cream.

Raspberry Jam *Raspberries have a high pectin content, and therefore make a well-set jam, one of*
the season's best. This is a treat through the winter months when summer is but a memory.

MAKES 2.5 KG (5 LB)

1.5 kg (3 lb) raspberries, washed and hulled

1 kg (2¼ lb) sugar

Toss the raspberries in the sugar in a big bowl, and leave in the sun until warmed through (this is advice from
an old country cookery book). Then slide the fruit and the juice that has formed into a pan, bring to the boil,
and cook rapidly to setting point (see page 145). Pot while still hot, and seal in the jars (see page 145).

A Seventeenth-Century RASPBERRY CREAM

Old-fashioned country 'creams' were in most cases fruit blended into a base of plain whipped cream,
sometimes lightened with beaten egg white. The colour of this one is beautiful – a clear 'apple blossom' effect. And the addition of rosewater is seductive:

When you have whipt your cream, sweeten it, and take two ladlefuls (only) and bruise the raspberries into
it, and season with rose-water, and again whip it well, and then put it to your [main] cream, and, stirring all
together, dish it up.

Ms of c.1700

Raspberry Vinegar *This is a 'must' for a well-stocked larder shelf. You can use it in salad dressings all the year round, and in delicately flavoured sauces. It is wonderful, and very easy to make.*

MAKES 3 LITRES (5 PINTS)

700 g (1½ lb) raspberries, washed and hulled

1.2 litres (2 pints) malt vinegar

1 kg (2¼ lb) sugar

Cover the raspberries with water, and simmer for 30 minutes. Strain off the juice into a large pan – there will be about 1.2 litres (2 pints). Add the vinegar and the sugar to the juice, and stir all together as it heats through. Bring to the boil, and simmer for 15–20 minutes, until the liquid becomes syrupy.

Pour into clean wine bottles and cork. Store in a cool, dark place.

Summer Trifle *This great classic of English cooking lends itself to improvisation with whatever fruits are in season. Traditionally, sherry was used to moisten the sponge.*

SERVES 6–8

16 trifle sponge cakes

150 ml (¼ pint) tropical fruit juice, or half and half with white wine

1.25 kg (2½ lb) mixed summer fruits, such as raspberries, strawberries, peaches, mangoes, kiwi fruit, grapes etc., prepared and sliced as necessary

40 g (1½ oz) caster sugar

600 ml (1 pint) thick custard or *Crème Anglaise* (see page 153)

600 ml (1 pint) thick Greek yoghurt

Cut the trifle sponge cakes in half lengthwise, and lay one third of them in the bottom of an attractive 20 cm (8 in) glass dish. Sprinkle one third of the tropical fruit juice or mixture of wine and juice over them, and set aside. Mix the prepared fruits with the sugar in another bowl, reserving a few raspberries and strawberries for decoration. Spoon half of the fruit with its juice over the sponges, and then repeat the layers, ending with a layer of sponge moistened with the last of the juice.

Mix the custard or *Crème Anglaise* with the Greek yoghurt, and spread it over the top. Chill overnight. Decorate with the reserved raspberries and strawberries, and serve.

Raspberry WATER ICE

Follow the recipe for Red or White Currant Water Ice on page 42, using 1.25 kg (2½ lb) raspberries, washed and hulled, instead of the mixture of currants and raspberries.

Currants Black, red and white currants are members of the Ribes

family. The blackcurrant, with its heavily scented leaves, grows wild across the whole of Europe and northern Asia. Its high vitamin content is greatly valued, and the shrub is now farmed extensively.

Red and white currants are found mainly by streams and in wet woodlands. The Scandinavians and Russians cultivate the redcurrant widely and it is a popular ingredient in their cooking. The white currant has its own distinctive flavour and is slightly less acidic than the red. Native to northern latitudes, the currant family was first cultivated in England in the early seventeenth century.

Red or White Currant Water Ice *Seventeenth-century cooks used to*

make little redcurrant creams (a version of syllabub without the wine), and a fool made with redcurrant juice was also popular. Sir Kenelm Digby recommended in 1669 that the redcurrants be 'fresh gathered' in the morning. This water ice is yet another delectable way of cooking with redcurrants, and makes an elegant dessert for a summer dinner-party.

SERVES 4–6

175 g (6 oz) sugar

150 ml (¼ pint) water

1 kg (2¼ lb) ripe red or white currants, washed and
   stripped from their stalks

225 g (8 oz) raspberries, washed and hulled

lemon juice to taste

Boil the sugar with the water for 6–8 minutes until syrupy. Purée the red or white currants and raspberries in a blender or food processor, and then pass through a sieve. Mix the resulting purée with the syrup, then add lemon juice to taste. Pour into a freezer container, cover and freeze for 1 hour, or until the edges begin to harden. Scoop out, and blend until smooth, then return to the freezer to complete the freezing. Alternatively, put the mixture into an ice-cream maker, and follow the manufacturer's instructions for freezing.

To convert this recipe into ice cream, purée the fruit but do not sieve. Then mix with sugar to sweeten or taste, or with syrup as above, and blend gradually with 600 ml (1 pint) 'fresh sweet cream' (i.e. *crème fraîche*), adding lemon juice only if desired. Fold in a beaten egg white, and freeze as above.

Blackcurrant JELLY

Blackcurrants gel very easily when ripe. The rich, thick juice of a deep, dark colour is, according to Eliza Acton (1840), 'useful in illness' and very refreshing.

If you have a juicer, treat yourself to this elixir of midsummer. To make blackcurrant jelly, follow the instructions for making jellies on page 146. Using 900 g (2 lb) fruit to 300 ml (½ pint) water, cover the pan and simmer for 30 minutes. Cool, then strain through a jelly bag.

To every 600 ml (1 pint) juice add 325 g (12 oz) granulated sugar. Stir over a gentle heat until the sugar has dissolved. Bring to the boil and boil rapidly to setting point, about 10 minutes. Remove scum as it arises.

Pour into warm, clean jars. Cover and seal.

Blackcurrant Flan
Based on the classic French technique of making fruit flans, this is hugely successful as a dessert for midsummer. The rich, slightly sharp flavour of the blackcurrants makes a mouthwatering contrast to the Crème Pâtissière *which lines a crisp pastry shell.*

SERVES 4–6

1½ recipe quantities Sweet Crust Pastry (see
 page 150)

1 recipe quantity *Crème Pâtissière* (see page 153)

700 g (1½ lb) blackcurrants, washed, topped and
 tailed

50 g (2 oz) caster sugar

4 tablespoons apricot jam

crème fraîche, to serve (optional)

Roll out the pastry, and use to line a 25 cm (10 in) greased flan tin. Bake blind (see page 152) in a preheated oven at 190°C/375°F/mark 5 for 20 minutes, until golden and firm. Cool. Spread the bottom with the *Crème Pâtissière*.

Put the prepared blackcurrants into a pan with the sugar, and heat gently, stirring carefully, for 3–4 minutes until the currants have softened slightly and the juice runs. Leave to cool in the pan, then strain off the juice, reserving it. Lay the currants over the *Crème Pâtissière*. Heat the apricot jam, adding enough of the reserved blackcurrant juice to make a pouring consistency, and strain it through a sieve. Trickle it over the blackcurrants. Leave to cool, and serve well chilled, with *crème fraîche* if desired.

Blackcurrant Clafoutis
Family food from the French, a clafoutis *consists of fresh fruit baked in a batter mixture. It rises to turn golden brown in the cooking, while the fruit inside melts in the mouth.*

SERVES 6

300 ml (½ pint) milk

50 g (2 oz) caster sugar

3 eggs

1 teaspoon vanilla essence

pinch of salt

100 g (4 oz) flour, sifted

450 g (1 lb) blackcurrants

25 g (1 oz) icing sugar

thick Greek yoghurt, to serve

Put all the ingredients except the fruit and icing sugar in a blender or food processor, and blend for 2 minutes to form a smooth batter. Pour a 6 mm (¼ inch) layer of the batter into the bottom of a greased 20 cm (8 in) square metal baking dish, and place over a moderate heat for a minute or so, swirling it around until a film of batter has set in the bottom of the dish. Be careful not to let it burn. Remove from the heat.

Spread the blackcurrants over the film of batter, and sprinkle on the icing sugar. Pour on the rest of the batter, place in the middle of a preheated oven, and bake at 180°C/350°F/mark 4 for 50–60 minutes, until puffed and brown, and when a sharp knife plunged into the centre comes out clean. Serve hot or warm (it will sink if not served immediately) with thick Greek yoghurt.

The Queen's SWEETMEAT

This appears to be a jelly of redcurrant and raspberry with whole cherries set in it. It sounds very special – worth a try if you are an inventive cook:

MARMULATE OF CHERRIES WITH JUICE OF RASPBERRIES AND CURRANTS: *Mingle juice of Rasps and red Currants with the stoned Cherries, and boil this mixture into Marmulate, with a quarter or at most a third part of Sugar ... Madam Plancy (who maketh this sweetmeat for the Queen) useth this proportion. Take three pounds of Cherries stoned: half a pound of clear juice of Raspes, and one pound of the juice of Red Currants, with one pound of fine Sugar. Put them all together in the preserving pan; boil them with a quick fire, especially at the first, skimming them all the while as any scum riseth. When you find them of a fit consistence, with a fine clear jelly mingled with the Cherries, take the preserving pan from the fire and bruise the Cherries with the back of your preserving spoon: put them up when they are of a fit temper of coolness, peradventure, to keep all the year, there may be requisite a little more Sugar.*

The Closet of Sir Kenelm Digby Opened, 1669

Gooseberries

The gooseberry is the first of our soft fruits to appear in the summer garden, and a gooseberry pie was traditionally served up at Whitsun celebrations in May. There is an old English recipe for such a pie in which the fruit and sugar are encased in a raised-pie crust – a sweet version of a pork-pie crust. When cooked, melted apple jelly was poured in through a slit in the lid and the pie was then left to set and gel. Other typically English recipes using gooseberries were for cakes, puddings, fools and jams, dishes which have stood the test of time and which are a distinctive part of English country cooking. Don't pick gooseberries too early in the season, though: unripe gooseberries are very sour and need a chance to sun ripen.

Whitsuntide Gooseberry Pie

Whitsuntide used to be celebrated as a major festival, with a Whitsun King and Queen chosen to preside over the fun. All over the land, parishioners gathered for various social events, and the first of the Morris dancers made their appearance in their ribbons and bells. The Sunday feast would end with a magnificent gooseberry pie.

SERVES 4–6

700 g (1½ lb) gooseberries, washed, topped and
 tailed

50–75 g (2–3 oz) caster sugar

⅔ recipe quantity Sweet Crust Pastry (see page 150)

1 egg white, beaten

thick Greek yoghurt or *Crème Anglaise* (see page
 153), to serve

Put the gooseberries into a large, shallow pie dish, and toss them in the sugar. Place an inverted egg cup in the centre. Roll out the pastry 6 mm (¼ in) thick, and cut it to fit over the top with a margin of about 9 mm (⅜ in). Moisten the rim of the dish, and place the pastry over the top. Press down the edges with a fork, and make a small slit in the centre above the egg cup. Decorate with pastry 'leaves' if you like, moistening the undersides of the 'leaves' before pressing them down. Brush with a beaten egg white, and bake in a preheated oven at 180°C/350°F/mark 4 for 25–30 minutes, until the pastry is set and turns a light golden colour. Serve hot, with lots of thick Greek yoghurt or *Crème Anglaise*.

Gooseberry Fool
Quintessentially English, the gooseberry fool is a delicate dish of subtle flavour, and an inimitable pale green colour. You can make it with cream or custard, depending on how rich you want it; or with thick Greek yoghurt for a sharper taste.

SERVES 4

450 g (1 lb) gooseberries, washed, topped and tailed

1 tablespoon butter

caster sugar to taste

300 ml (½ pint) whipping cream, thick Greek
   yoghurt or custard

thin, crisp biscuits, to serve

Put the gooseberries into a baking dish with a little water, cover with a lid and bake in a preheated oven at 170°C/325°F/mark 3, until completely soft and pulpy, about 40–45 minutes. Alternatively, you can microwave them. While they are still hot, stir in the butter and enough sugar to sweeten. Cool, then purée in a blender or food processor. Sieve them if you want a very fine fool.

Whip the cream, if using, to the same consistency as the fool, or use thick Greek yoghurt or custard, and fold it softly into the purée. Spoon into glasses, and chill thoroughly. Serve with thin, crisp biscuits.

Gooseberry and Elderflower Compote
The name 'gooseberry' means 'crisp berry', and the shrub grows successfully only in fairly northerly climes. Gooseberries thrive in the Midlands, and also in Scotland, the Shetland Islands and Orkney. They have therefore not been much used in European cuisines, but the British have many traditional recipes which make use of them. This one links the gooseberry with the elderflower, two distinctly compatible flavours.

SERVES 3–4

100 g (4 oz) sugar

300 ml (½ pint) water

450 g (1 lb) gooseberries, washed, topped and tailed

2 elderflower heads, tied in a muslin bag

crisp biscuits, to serve

Make a syrup by dissolving the sugar in the water and boiling it for 5 minutes. Add the gooseberries to the syrup, with the elderflowers, and cook very gently for 10 minutes, partially covered. Remove the elderflowers and cool the gooseberries. Chill. Serve in glass bowls, with delicate crisp biscuits to hand around.

Gooseberry and Elderflower Jam *Even when you use green*

gooseberries, as opposed to the red dessert ones, this jam turns a dark pink when finally cooked. The muscatel fragrance of the elderflower gives it a unique flavour. A wonderful summer jam, it is excellent on freshly baked bread or scones, and delicious as a filling for a plain sponge cake.

MAKES 3 KG (7 LB)

1.5 kg (3 lb) gooseberries, washed, topped and
    tailed

1.2 litres (2 pints) water

4 large elderflower heads, tied in a muslin bag

2 kg (4 lb) sugar

Simmer the gooseberries in the water with the bag of elderflowers for 30 minutes. Remove the elderflowers, add the sugar and stir until dissolved. Boil to setting point (see page 145). Pot in warm, clean jars, cover and seal (see page 145). Store in a cool, dark place.

Groseillee *This is a raspberry and gooseberry jelly which, at a guess from its name, is of French*

inspiration. The French use gooseberries very little in their cooking – perhaps because it is not a native plant – although their gooseberry sauce for mackerel is well known. This combination of fruits, however, is inspired.

MAKES 2 KG (4 LB)

1.5 kg (3 lb) gooseberries, washed, topped and
    tailed

450 g (1 lb) raspberries, washed and hulled

sugar

Raspberry Juice:

325 g (12 oz) raspberries, washed and hulled

600 ml (1 pint) water

Put the gooseberries and raspberries into a preserving pan with water to cover. Boil for 10 minutes, then strain through a jelly bag for several hours (see page 146) into the cleansed pan.

Meanwhile, make the raspberry juice: place the raspberries and water in a pan and simmer, covered, for 20 minutes. Strain the juice, discarding the contents of the sieve.

Add the raspberry juice to the pan, and boil briskly for 30 minutes. Measure, and add 325 g (12 oz) sugar to every 600 ml (1 pint) of liquid. Dissolve the sugar over a medium heat, then boil for a further 15 minutes or until setting point is reached (see page 145). Pour into warm, clean jars, cover and seal (see page 145). Store in a cool, dark place.

Mulberries In the garden where I spent part of my childhood, a spectacular mulberry tree spread its low branches over the small lawn. This heavy canopy covered the grass, which in summer became encrusted with shining, dark red berries. As the fruit ripened, pools of staining purple marked the grass. If you picked the fruit, your fingers were immediately marked with a purplish-red dye which was difficult to remove, and woe betide you if the juice dribbled down your clothing, as it was prone to do, since the ripe fruit spurts its 'blood' when you bite into it.

Mulberry Pie *Mulberry trees were planted in some considerable numbers where a silk industry thrived, and it is interesting how many are still found in gardens in and around London. If you are lucky enough to lay your hands on supplies of this wonderful berry with its crisp texture and fountains of juice, try making this fruit pie. It is exceptional.*

SERVES 4

2 medium apples, peeled, cored and sliced

caster sugar to taste

a pinch of ground cinnamon

450 g (1 lb) mulberries, washed and hulled

100 g (4 oz) shop-bought puff pastry

1 egg, beaten

whipped cream or *Crème Anglaise* (see page 153), to serve

Place the apple slices over the bottom of a shallow, buttered pie dish, and sprinkle with a little caster sugar and a pinch of cinnamon. Toss the mulberries in some caster sugar, and spread over the apples.

Roll the pastry out to 6 mm (¼ inch) thick and cut it to fit the top of the dish, allowing for a margin of about 9 mm (⅜ inch). Moisten the rim of the dish, lay the pastry over the top, and press the edges down with a fork. Cut a few simple flower or petal shapes out of the pastry scraps, moisten the undersides, and press them lightly on to the top as decoration. Brush with the beaten egg. Bake in a preheated oven at 200°C/400°F/mark 6 for 10 minutes, then turn the heat down to 170°C/325°F/mark 3, and bake for a further 10–15 minutes until well risen and golden. Serve hot with cream or *Crème Anglaise*.

herbs and *Flowers*

Speak not – whisper not;

Here bloweth thyme and bergamot;

Softly on the evening hour,

Secret herbs their spices shower,

Dark-spiked rosemary and myrrh,

Lean-stalked, purple lavender;

Hides within her bosom, too,

All her sorrows, bitter rue.

A Child's Garden, **Walter de la Mare (1873–1956)**

A herb garden has its own special beauty. The variety of foliage colour, delightful flowers and above all the fragrances combine to please the senses, and also do much to attract butterflies and bees throughout the summer. Herbs were originally cultivated as 'useful plants', for medicinal, culinary and cosmetic purposes. The herbal tradition is as old as civilization, and the first herb gardens in Europe were planted for monastic infirmaries. Archetypal monastic gardens were little cloisters whose ruins are witness to their past, as are the illustrations in illuminated manuscripts. Such a herb garden might have been walled or hedged around, and placed in a sunny, sheltered position next to the infirmary. Neatly laid out in beds, there would be walkways between the rows of plants to inhale their aromas.

HERBS AS MEDICINE

Anglo-Saxon herbals list about 500 plants used in medicine and for the recovery of the sick. Our word 'drug' comes from the Anglo-Saxon *driggen*, to dry (the herbs). Thus herbs were among the necessities of life, alongside the vegetable patch, vines and fruits in the orchard, chickens and bees. Used primarily for healing and flavouring, some herbs also yielded useful dyes for inks and fabrics, others fragrances for incense.

Infirmary herbs included sage, whose generic name comes from the Latin meaning 'to be in good health'. Traditionally the first meal given to a monk after sickness and blood-letting was sage and parsley in a dish of soft eggs. 'He that would live for aye must eat sage in May', goes an old English proverb. Clary sage was used

as an eyewash, and hyssop as a metabolic stimulant as well as a strewing herb, loved for its sweet resinous orange scent. Rue found its place in holy water and as an air cleanser – to be found in posies in the Law Courts up until the eighteenth century. Chamomile was fondly known as the 'plants' physician', a good companion plant which also made a fragrant lawn. Dill was found to soothe the digestive system, and borage to cheer the melancholy. All these herbs were used in infusions, or in food, or as strewing herbs to impart their various qualities. Bunches of herbs were gathered at the height of their pungency, and dried in bunches hanging from beams and rafters, to preserve them for the year ahead.

The Cottage Garden

Later, as gardening evolved, formal herb gardens came into their own: herbs lend themselves to garden design because many are hardy, quick growers, and several are evergreen. They also look delightful integrated amongst border plants, giving a cottage garden effect that has echoes in our rural past. The cottager, like the monks, would grow particular herbs with a view to their usefulness for country medicine, for tisanes and cooking, as bee plants, or for all these reasons.

By the sixteenth century the cottager now had his own garden in addition to an allotment acreage, and this was to become the woman's domain. Thomas Tusser's *100 Good Points of Husbandry* (1557) recommends dozens of herbs and seeds for the garden, as well as up to 40 for decoration. He makes clear that both cottager and his wife must 'moile and toile' in order to keep a good table and to be prosperous. So he outlines a list of herbs for the kitchen, for teas and tisanes, for salads and sauces, or to boil and butter. He catalogues strewing herbs, herbs and flowers for window-sills and pots, herbs for the still, and medicinal plants which were also often used as household antiseptics.

Under the umbrella term 'herbs' are listed garden plants, wild flowers, soft fruits and some vegetables: a 'herbe' meant a pungent or aromatic plant which had its place anywhere in the garden or orchard, so the average cottage garden remained a patch where old-fashioned vegetables, fruit, flowers and herbs mingled in glorious abandon. They were used fresh in spring and summer, and dried for use throughout the winter months.

Decorative Herbs

As garden design became more sophisticated, decorative herb gardens – as distinct from useful ones – came into being: they came into the sights of the rich, the leisured and the dedicated horticulturist. One common factor remained, however, which was that herbs were still the pastime of the woman of the house: hers were the medicinal and culinary skills, and literature is strewn with references to women herbalists.

Among favourite garden herbs was the dramatic angelica, tall and stately. Lavender was grown for its inimitable fragrance, as well as being used in cordials, preserves and lavender water. Lemon balm was, and still is, the classic 'bee plant', and makes a wonderful herb tea. Basil, the sweetest of herbs, was used for cooking as well as aromatics, and marjoram and thyme were omnipresent. Mint maintained its reputation from ancient times, in all its varieties and forms, as a cure-all. It was still sometimes called 'monks' herb', from its prominence in old infirmary gardens. Savory, coriander and caraway were found to be good border plants as well as excellent culinary herbs, and used to spice wine and cakes.

HERB LORE: ROSEMARY

Herbs for the kitchen garden then, as now, included parsley, chervil, lovage, tansy and – a huge favourite – rosemary. 'The perfect herb', it arrived in England around 1338 and acquired more folklore than any of its peers – for example, that it reaches 33 years of age and never exceeds either Christ's age or his height (the height of a man and a half). Rosemary's reputation acquired a Christian edge: it healed with His compassion, it purified with His grace, and got its mist-blue flowers from the Virgin Mary spreading her cloak over a rosemary bush to dry. A rosemary branch, gilded and tied with silk ribbons, was also presented to wedding guests as a symbol of love and loyalty. Together with an orange stuck with cloves it was given as a New Year's gift.

The medievals liked to 'seethe rosmarie in wine ... and thou shalt be merry and lythe'. Rosemary tea calmed and 'cleansed the body within ... and wash thy visage well therein, it shall make thee whole and clear... For it is kindly ... for it is holy' says a fourteenth-century manuscript. Principally, though, rosemary is for remembrance, memorably quoted by Ophelia to Hamlet, and there is an ancient custom of burying the dead with a sprig of rosemary. Sir Thomas More, in a letter to his daughter Margaret, paid his tribute in the sixteenth century: *As for Rosmarie, I lett it runne all over my garden walls, not onlie because my bees love it, but because it is a herb sacred to remembrance, and, therefore, to friendship; whence a sprig of it hath a dumb language that maketh it the chosen emblem of our funeral wakes and in our burial grounds.*

CULINARY HERBS

Cooking with herbs is an extension of the pleasure of herb gardening. Herbs have their place in the greatest of the world's gastronomic dishes. They are distinctive and versatile, a joy to make salads with as well as to cook with, and they fill the house with their aromas as you work with them in the kitchen.

The flowers of all the herbs mentioned on the following pages, and many wild and garden plants, make elegant edible garnishes, and sometimes flavourings, for summer food. This is a guide to which flowers to use, their colours and flavours. Many are wonderful in salads, some in vinegars, others in ice creams and fruit desserts. They are as much a delight to the palate as a pleasure to the eye. The recipes which follow highlight beautifully the qualities of the herbs used in them.

Marjoram Olives
Closely related to oregano, marjoram was known to the ancient Greeks as 'joy of the mountain': Aphrodite, they told, took it from the depths of the ocean to the tops of the highest peaks, where it could grow close to the sun. It is a symbol of peace and happiness.

Indeed, Sir, she was the sweet marjoram of the Salad, or rather the herb of grace.

William Shakespeare

YOU WILL NEED: • **sprigs of marjoram** • **black olives** • **olive oil**

Put the marjoram into a tall jam jar, and add enough olives to come two-thirds of the way up the jar. Top up with good quality olive oil, and shake well. Seal, and store in a cool, dark place.

Leave for several days, or up to several weeks, and the olives will take on the fragrance of the herb. When you have eaten all the olives, decant the oil and use it in salad dressings for tomatoes, beetroot or potatoes – vegetables that can take strong flavours.

Fresh Herb Soup
A summer soup full of the flavours of fresh herbs is one of the delights of the season, evocative of the time when herbs are at their best and most aromatic: May and early June are the months to make the most of these highly aromatic, tender leaves.

SERVES 4

40 g (1½oz) butter or margarine

25 g (1 oz) plain flour

1 litre (1¾ pints) Vegetable Stock (see page 154)

100 g (4 oz) herb leaves, such as lovage, parsley, sage, fennel, thyme, marjoram, balm etc., chopped

225 g (8 oz) potatoes, cooked and sliced

salt and freshly ground black pepper

2 tablespoons *crème fraîche* or yoghurt

herb flowers, to garnish

Melba Toast (see page 155), to serve

Melt the butter or margarine in a large pan, and stir in the flour. Gradually add half the stock, stirring constantly until smooth, and bring to the boil. Add the herb leaves, and simmer gently for 5 minutes. Add the potatoes, simmer for a further 5 minutes and then purée in the blender or food processor. Add the rest of the stock, season to taste and finally stir in the *crème fraîche* or yoghurt. Garnish with a few herb flowers, and serve with Melba Toast.

Gazpacho

This is my personal version of a great Spanish classic: a chilled, uncooked tomato soup. If you grow lovage, use young leaves early in the season for their inimitable flavour; balance this with delicate chervil, and add chives for 'bite'. These three tastes linger on the palate, and make this herby gazpacho a memorable starter for long summer evenings.

SERVES 4

700 g (1½ lb) tomatoes

50 g (2 oz) fresh breadcrumbs

475 g (15 oz) can tomato juice

2 canned sweet peppers, drained and chopped

1 large clove garlic, peeled and finely chopped

3–4 tablespoons olive oil

½ small Spanish onion, very finely chopped

1 small cucumber, peeled and grated

1 tablespoon each finely chopped fresh lovage,
  chervil and chives

salt and freshly ground black pepper

2 tablespoons Mayonnaise (see page 122)

To Garnish:

chopped black olives and hard-boiled eggs

Croûtons (see page 155)

Skin the tomatoes (see page 102). Chop roughly, and remove any woody parts. Blend to a smooth purée with the breadcrumbs, canned tomato juice, chopped peppers, garlic and olive oil. Stir in the onion, cucumber and herbs, and season to taste. Stir in the Mayonnaise to make the soup creamy. Chill thoroughly, and serve with a decorative dish of the garnishes.

Herb Bread

The wonderful aromas of this bread fill the house as it cooks – imagine the smell of fresh yeast dough and fresh herbs drifting out of the oven! It is a perfect bread for a simple summer lunch alfresco, to go with the Crème Vichyssoise *on page 78. Good cheeses and some fresh fruits of the season would turn it into a feast.*

MAKES A 700 G (1½ LB) LOAF

225 g (8 oz) each wholemeal and plain unbleached
  flour, sifted

7 g (¼ oz) margarine

2 teaspoons each salt and sugar

1 teaspoon dill seed

2 teaspoons chopped fresh savory or marjoram

1 teaspoon chopped fresh dill

15 g (½ oz) fresh yeast or 2 teaspoons active
  dried yeast

300 ml (½ pint) warm water

Mix the flours, and rub in the margarine. Add the salt, sugar, dill seed and herbs, and mix well. Blend the fresh yeast, if using, in the warm water, and when it has dissolved add all at once to the flour mixture. Mix to a soft scone-like dough so that it leaves the bowl clean.

If you are using dried yeast, dissolve it in a little of the water with 1 teaspoon of the sugar first, and leave for 10 minutes until frothy. Add with the remaining water to the flour mixture, and again mix well to form the dough.

Knead the dough thoroughly on a lightly floured board. Put into a 900g (2 lb) loaf tin, previously greased and sprinkled with bulgar wheat. Place in a warm place, covered with a towel or inside a plastic bag, until the dough doubles in volume, about 2–3 hours. Bake in a preheated oven at 230°C/450°F/mark 8 for 30–40 minutes. Serve still warm from the oven, with soup, or as a bread and cheese lunch with salad (see Cottage Garden Salad below).

Cottage Garden Salad *Pungent mint is an excellent taste for summer salads, and if lemon balm grows abundantly in your garden, as it does in mine, they complement each other well. Parsley, often overlooked and perceived as ordinary, is nothing of the sort in a salad like this, with its strong, earthy flavour. Choose your own selection from the herb patch, and enjoy the freshness of this garden salad.*

SERVES 2–3

1 crisp lettuce, washed and shredded

2 baby carrots, scrubbed and diced

75 g (3 oz) red cabbage, washed and finely shredded

100 g (4 oz) shelled garden peas, lightly cooked

1 shallot, finely chopped

2 tomatoes, chopped

2 courgettes, thinly sliced and lightly cooked

a handful of alfalfa sprouts

a handful of chopped mixed fresh herbs, such as chervil, mint, balm, parsley and other favourites

1 recipe quantity Vinaigrette (see page 155), made with a Flower Vinegar (see page 58), to dress

nasturtium flowers, to decorate

Mix all the salad ingredients together in a big bowl. Dress with the Vinaigrette, and decorate with nasturtium flowers. Serve with Herb Bread (see opposite).

Sallet of ALL KINDS OF HERBS

TO MAKE A SALLET OF ALL KINDS OF HERBS: *Take your Herbs (as the tops of red Sage, Mint, Lettuce, Violets, Marigold, Spinach etcetera) and pick them very fine in fair water: and wash your flowers by them-selves, and swing them in a strainer. Then mingle them in a dish with Cucumbers and Lemons pared and sliced; scrape thereon Sugar and put Vinegar and Oil. Spread your Flowers on top of the Sallet, and take Eggs boiled hard and lay them about the dish.*

A book of Flowers and Fruit, Thomas Jenner, 1653

Summer Salad

Fennel and thyme are two great favourites in my herb garden. Fennel's fine feathery leaves have an aniseedy taste, and are said to impart stamina and strength as well as being good for slimmers. Thyme, so fragrant that it used to be used for incense, still grows on Mount Hymettus as it did in the days of classical Greece, and makes legendary honey: 'Homey mistresses and such as keep bees hope to have a good yeare, when they see the Time to bloom abundantly,' John Gerard tells us in his Herbal *of 1597. The combined flavours of these two herbs make an unforgettable summer salad.*

SERVES 2–3

1 small, crisp, green lettuce, washed and shredded

1 red lettuce (oak leaf or *lollo rosso*), washed and
  dried

175 g (6 oz) small cauliflower florets

2 stalks celery, trimmed and sliced

2 carrots, peeled and cut into matchsticks

6 cherry tomatoes, halved

4 radishes, trimmed and sliced

2 tablespoons each chopped fresh fennel and thyme

1 yellow pepper, seeded and cut into strips

1 small bunch watercress or sweet rocket, washed
  and dried

1 recipe quantity Vinaigrette (see page 155), made
  with a Flower Vinegar (see below), to dress

flower petals to decorate

Put the green lettuce into the bottom of a large bowl, and arrange the red leaves around the edge. Place the rest of the salad ingredients, mixed together, into the centre. Just before serving, trickle the Vinaigrette over the top, and decorate with flower petals of your choice – stocks petals are among my favourites in high summer.

Herb or Flower VINEGAR

Any of the following give a subtle flavour to vinegars, delightful in salad dressings throughout the summer: roses, violets, elderflowers, nasturtiums, lavender, rosemary, tarragon and thyme. You will need one handful of the herb/flower to every 600 ml (1 pint) good quality white wine vinegar.

Remove the stems, and the green and white 'heels' from the flowers and petals, and make sure that the leaves and flowers are clean and perfectly dry. Use wide-necked jars or bottles for the bigger plants.

Place the herb or flowers in a clean bottle or jar, and fill up with the vinegar. Seal, leave to stand on a sunny window-sill for about 2 weeks, before straining off the vinegar and bottling it.

Right: *Summer salad*

Italian Dip
*This gentle dip has a soft texture and bland, earthy flavours dominated by parsley. Parsley was a symbol of strength to the Greeks and, indeed, it is full of nutritious goodness: Vitamins A, B and C, large amounts of iron and calcium, and many minerals. But there is a proverb from Spanish folklore which warns against eating too much parsley, otherwise you will look older than your years! So balance it in this dip with sweet marjoram, a 'settling' herb, which John Gerard (*Herbal, *1597) tells us, 'is very good against the warmbling of the stomach'.*

SERVES 4

1 medium aubergine

1 medium bunch fresh parsley, chopped

1 medium bunch fresh marjoram, chopped

½ canned red pepper, seeded and chopped

3 tablespoons olive oil

squeeze of lemon juice

salt and freshly ground black pepper

tortilla chips or crudités, to serve

Put the aubergine into boiling water and simmer for 20 minutes, or until completely soft. Cool, then skin. Put the flesh into a blender or food processor with the chopped parsley, marjoram, red pepper and olive oil. Blend to a dipping consistency. Add a little lemon juice, and season to taste. Serve with tortilla chips or similar spicy snacks, and crudités of your choice.

Pesto Sauce
Pesto is one of the world's best sauces for pasta, and you can also use it to dress a tomato salad, or a crisp green salad with croûtons. In short, you can improvise endlessly, not only with how to use it, but also with how to make it. The classic pesto is made with basil, garlic, pine nuts, olive oil and Parmesan cheese. Basil, to the ancients, was the king of herbs, and in India it was made sacred to the god Vishnu. John Gerard tells us in his Herbal *of 1597 that 'the smell of Basil is good for the heart... It taketh away sorrowfulness, which cometh of melancholy and maketh a man merry and glad'. But there is no reason not to experiment with other nuts and herbs. For example, parsley with walnuts, tarragon with hazelnuts, or dill with almonds. So substitute them accordingly, following this basic method:*

1 large bunch fresh basil, chopped

2 cloves garlic, peeled and crushed

50 g (2 oz) pine nuts

150 ml (¼ pint) olive oil

25 g (1 oz) Parmesan cheese

sea salt

Blend the basil, garlic and pine nuts with half of the olive oil in the blender or food processor, until smooth. Stir in the rest of the oil and the Parmesan, and season with a little sea salt if necessary.

Herb MAYONNAISE

Add 2 tablespoons very finely chopped fresh tarragon to the Mayonnaise on page 122, and leave to stand for at least 2 hours before serving. Other herbs which make excellent Herb Mayonnaise are:

- chives
- parsley
- marjoram
- basil
- coriander
- savory – or a judicious mixture of *fines herbes* – according to taste.

Flower Ice Cream
Flowers were used far more frequently in the old days than they are today – yet they are wonderful both for flavour and to decorate dishes. This ice cream is simply amazing, a scented, delicate and creamy dessert which makes an elegant end to a summer's day. The best petals to use are undoubtedly well-scented roses, or stocks and honeysuckle: your senses will reel!

SERVES 4

300 ml (½ pint) double cream

½ teacup full of scented petals

½ teaspoon orangeflower water

2 eggs, separated

75 g (3 oz) caster sugar

extra petals, to decorate

Heat the cream gently, and stir in the petals. Leave to stand over a pan of hot water (not boiling) for 10–15 minutes to allow the petals to infuse. Keep it covered. Then allow to cool completely before adding the orangeflower water. Strain.

Beat the cream until thick. Beat the egg yolks with the sugar until thick and pale yellow, and then fold in the cream. Beat the egg whites until very stiff, and fold them in. Put into a freezer container, cover and freeze for 1 hour. Remove from the freezer, blend until smooth, then cover and return to the freezer for the final freezing. Alternatively, use an ice-cream maker, and follow the manufacturer's instructions.

Serve in scoops, slightly softened, and decorate each helping with fresh petals.

the vegetable *Patch*

Then a sentimental passion of vegetable fashion must excite your languid spleen,

An attachment à la Plato for a bashful young potato, or a not too French French bean!

Though the Philistines may jostle, you will rank as an apostle in the high aesthetic band,

If you walk down Piccadilly with a poppy or a lily in your medieval hand.

And everyone will say,

As you walk your flowery way,

'If he's content with a vegetable love which would certainly not suit me,

Why, what a most particularly pure young man this pure young man must be!'

Patience, **W. S. Gilbert, 1881**

The basic vegetables of medieval England were indeed basic. A twelfth-century treatise gives a clue: 'In a kitchen there should be a small table on which cabbage may be minced, and also lentils, peas, shelled beans, beans in the pod, millet, onions and other vegetables of the kind that can be cut up.' The fact is that the medieval palate was not highly tuned to the delicacy of vegetables as we know them today: they liked them to be either starchy or strong in flavour, and always as a small supplement to a diet largely carnivorous, backed up by bread, cheese and ale. This humble culinary tradition reflected the lifestyle of the majority: a simple rural economy prevailed, based on a two-tiered class system, untouched in those early days by the demands of fashion that are so imperative today.

The cottager, who represented the majority of the English population, had a little 'yard' rather than a gar-

den, in which fruit trees, vegetables, herbs and flowers all grew together, well manured by the resident live-stock, household slops and privy, vegetable refuse and chimney soot. Chickens scratched around, maybe there was a beehive, perhaps geese and ducks as well, and some cottagers kept a pig. Field strips allowed the householder to supplement his food supply and kept him in enough peas and beans to see him through the winter. The bean, especially, was ubiquitous because of its food value, and a symbol of necessary wealth: our saying, 'I haven't got a bean', grew out of a medieval proverb. Edward Lear exercised his limerick skills on this humble subject:

There was an old person of Dean
Who dined on one pea and one bean;
For he said, 'More than that
Would make me too fat.'
That cautious old person of Dean.

Book of Nonsense, Edward Lear, 1846

The Anglo-Saxon word for a gardener was a 'leek-ward', indicating their preference for strong tastes, which also accounts for their use of pungent herbs, both cultivated and wild. Chaucer's Summoner in *The Canterbury Tales* (*c.*1387) 'well loved ... garlic onions and eke [moreover] leeks'. The leek was the winter vegetable or pot-herb *par excellence*, intro-duced by the Romans to England, and the *Allium* family in general became the stock-in-trade of English peasant cookery. Records of 1333 from Glastonbury Abbey show that they produced 5,000 cloves of garlic that year. Garlic sauce with goose on Sundays was a traditional feast for those who had the resources.

But overall the medieval countryman didn't bother much with vegetables. They were used mainly in soup, and for boiling up with meat in the 'pot' – especially with bacon. Even on the tables of the rich they made rel-atively rare appearances. Vegetables and herbs were used on fasting days in the monasteries, and the cabbage was ubiquitous. Generally it was cooked from dawn until dusk, almost to a purée, then heavily spiced with salt, mustard, garlic or vinegar. The name 'cabbage' comes from the medieval 'caboche', derived from the Latin *caput*, head. By the fifteenth century the bourgeois classes were treating cabbages as individual vege-tables, and served them buttered – although the smartest and most affluent ate cabbage as a salad vegetable.

Vegetables are to some extent a social barometer; they tell quite a lot about aspects of living at any given period among different social groups. As trade and travel began to open up in the sixteenth century, so accord-ingly did the appearance of vegetables on the table. By the mid-sixteenth century Thomas Tusser, in his *100 Good Points of Husbandry* of 1557, lists asparagus, beans, beets, cabbage, carrots, cucumber, globe artichokes, gourds, leeks, onions, parsnips, peas, pumpkin, radishes, skirret, spinach and turnips. There was no mention yet of potatoes and tomatoes, which did not arrive on the scene until the end of the century.

A quarter of an acre was long thought to be a suitable size plot on which a man could cultivate enough to feed his family well, and by the seventeenth century the list had expanded to include Windsor beans, scarlet runners, early potatoes, Prussian Potatoes, Devonshire potatoes, radishes, Cos lettuce, barley – and tobacco! Families would supplement their diet with wild vegetables and herbs such as hop-tops, fat hen, nettles and sorrel, and the canny would plant sloe for hedging, so that they could make sloe gin in the autumn for winter consumption. High hedges of crab apple of great antiquity can still be seen in parts of England, planted for a similar dual purpose: the hedge supplied the larder shelf.

By the eighteenth century, once the potato had become established in Britain, it became a delicacy for the rich man's table, often cooked with spices or even candied. Onions and artichokes had been mentioned by John Parkinson in his *Paradisi in Sole* of 1620, along with the regular medieval pot herbs – including turnips, described as 'a poor man's feast, very windy'. A century later, a stately garden would include a walled vegetable garden with gravel paths and rustic arch, and the gardener grew mushrooms and asparagus alongside melons, vines and strawberries. But for poorer folk things stayed much the same: in *Our Village*, written in the 1820s, Miss Mitford mentions all the fruits, but doesn't deem vegetables worthy of mention. It was taken as read that onions, leeks, root vegetables, cabbage, peas, carrots and salad vegetables were grown, but these were too ordinary to be noteworthy. Yet Gilbert White, author of *The Natural History of Selbourne*, 1789, attributed the decline of leprosy in Britain to a general increase in the eating of vegetables! However, although Wordsworth sowed scarlet runner beans in his garden, it is said that his favourite place to be was in the orchard.

By Wordsworth's time, allotment gardens were beginning to catch on. Even though the first Act of Parliament had been passed in 1819, the idea had not enjoyed instant success, since the concept of a strip of land, not attached to the house, of about a quarter of an acre, for those who could afford the rent, did not have popular appeal. It took time to engage into the social fabric but, once established, it became a popular and socially important phenomenon, which persists into modern life.

The second half of the twentieth century has seen an ever-increasing interest in vegetables, and a marked change in their cooking and usage. Vegetables came to be respected in their own right, often cooked with enticing flavourings and spices, influenced by ethnic cultures from around the world. As ever a gauge of social and cultural change, the expansion of worldwide food markets has led to the appearance of exotic vegetables from all corners of the globe on the supermarket shelf. Whereas in the 1950s the greengrocer would boast little more than Tusser's catalogue for its regular produce, today the display is wide-ranging, bright and intriguing. A rise in vegetarianism has embraced this development, and the two have been mutually supportive: vegetarian cooking came out of its brown-rice-and-sandals image into a world of inspired and creative cuisine, motivated not least by a growing concern among the public for a healthy diet. This makes it all the more satisfying to grow your own fresh vegetables for use the year round. The flavour of newly gathered garden produce is incomparably better than commercially produced vegetables, and a well-thought-out vegetable patch can keep you in food throughout the year.

Potatoes The potato was discovered in the New World by the

Conquistadores, and grown in botanical gardens in Spain, although to start with not many people were interested in eating them. The Irish were the first to consume them on a large scale. Not until the nineteenth century did England and Scotland start to cultivate them widely, followed by France.

These potatoes be the most delicate rootes that may be eaten, and doe farre exceed our parseneps or carets. Their pines be of the bignes of two fists, the outside whereof is of the making of a pine-apple, but it is soft like the rinde of a Cucumber, and the inside eateth like an apple but it is more delicious than any sweet apple sugred.

Sir Francis Drake, late sixteenth century

Colcannon *By the end of the seventeenth century potatoes were the most important food crop in Ireland. 'Colcannon' is a typically Irish way of cooking them.*

SERVES 4

700 g (1½ lb) potatoes, peeled and boiled until
   tender

8 spring onions, trimmed and sliced

150 ml (¼ pint) hot milk

50 g (2 oz) butter or margarine

325 g (12 oz) outer cabbage leaves, shredded and
   cooked

salt and freshly ground black pepper

Drain the potatoes, and dry them quickly over a gentle heat, tossing in the pan. Set to one side. Pour boiling water over the spring onions in a bowl to soften them. Drain, and heat them gently with the milk for 5–6 minutes. Mash the potatoes, and beat the milk mixture in until soft and light.

Melt the butter or margarine in a pan, and toss the shredded cabbage in it. Fold into the potato. Season generously. You can serve it as it is, or fry it in butter, oil or dripping like a thick pancake, until the outside is crusty, crisp and brown (see Fried Potato Cake on page 68).

Potato SALAD

There are endless variations on the theme of potato salad. It is best to use waxy, young potatoes – the floury ones do not make good salads. Slice, season and dress them while still warm. Improvisation is the name of the game:

• with chopped raw onions in mayonnaise

• in vinaigrette, with chopped chives

• with strips of grilled pepper and green olives, in mayonnaise

• with celery and fresh herbs, having sprinkled some white wine over the potatoes while still warm. Dress with a light mayonnaise

• with artichoke hearts and salsify and rosemary, in mayonnaise

Fried Potato Cake
Potatoes are always substantial and nourishing, and this fried potato cake or hash conjures memories of childhood for me, supper food on bleak winter evenings.

YOU WILL NEED: • dripping or oil • leftover cooked potatoes, roughly mashed

Melt some dripping or oil in a deep, thick-bottomed frying pan. When it is smoking, press in the potatoes. Turn the heat down a little. As the bottom browns, keep stirring it from the bottom until the mass is full of fried brown pieces. Then press it all down firmly, and leave to cook over a gentle heat for 10–15 minutes until the bottom is evenly browned and crusty. Invert on to a platter to serve.

Parsnips
The parsnip is cultivated throughout the northern hemisphere. Parsnip tops have been fed to pigs and cattle for centuries: 'In October, the leaves of the parsnips should be given to cows... They will impart much richness to the milk,' says Lawson's *Agricultural Manual* of 1858. They have therefore invited ridicule from those who are not enamoured of them, although parsnips are a versatile and delicate vegetable. Their sweet flavour was extremely popular in medieval times, plus the useful fact that they could stay in the ground over winter. Parsnips are best eaten after the first frost, since then the flavour becomes more mellow.

Parsnip Chips *Parsnips are perhaps best loved in English cookery roasted alongside potatoes with the Sunday joint. Here is another popular way of cooking them, just like potato chips. They melt in the mouth.*

YOU WILL NEED: • **parsnips** • **oil for deep-frying**

Wash and scrape sufficient parsnips for your meal, and cut each into four wedges. Keep dividing these wedges until you have pieces about the thickness of a pencil. Put into enough cold water to cover, and bring to the boil. Cook for 2–3 minutes. Drain, and dry on a clean cloth.

Heat the oil in a deep pan or deep-fat fryer until smoking, and fry the chips until crisp and golden. Drain on absorbent kitchen paper, and pile high on to a hot platter. These, with baked autumn tomatoes and dripping toast, make a country supper in themselves.

Curried Parsnip Soup *Parsnips make a wonderful, warming, winter soup, especially when spiced with hot curry flavours which are an excellent foil to the sweetness of the vegetable. This soup makes a satisfying lunch served with warm wholemeal bread and butter.*

SERVES 3–4

1 medium onion, peeled and chopped

1 large parsnip, peeled and chopped

2 tablespoons butter or margarine

1 tablespoon flour

1–2 teaspoons curry paste

1.2 litres (2 pints) Vegetable Stock (see page 154)

150 ml (¼ pint) cream (optional)

1 tablespoon chopped fresh parsley

salt and freshly ground black pepper

Croûtons (see page 155), to serve

Cook the chopped onion and parsnip gently in the butter or margarine, covered, for 10 minutes, stirring so that they do not brown but become soft and sweet. Stir in the flour and curry paste to taste. Cook for 2 minutes, stirring, then pour in the stock gradually. Simmer until the parsnips are tender, 5–8 minutes more. Blend to a fine purée in a blender or food processor. Add more stock if necessary, or cream if you prefer. Stir in the chopped fresh parsley. Heat through, but do not let boil, and adjust the seasoning. Serve the soup with Croûtons.

Turnips
There is a saying, 'not worth a withered neep', which describes the generally low opinion of the humble turnip: you have to be hungry to bother with it. But the further north you go, the more popular, it seems, does this earth-flavoured root become. Turnips are best eaten young, before their flavour becomes too strong.

Glazed Turnips
Young turnips, lightly cooked so that they are still crisp, then sautéed in butter with a little sugar, make a delectable side dish to go with roast chicken or game birds.

SERVES 2

450 g (1 lb) younger turnips, peeled and cut into 2 cm (¾ in) dice

salt

a good knob of butter

2 tablespoons sugar

Blanch the turnips in boiling salted water until cooked but still slightly crisp. Drain. Melt the butter in a heavy pan, and put the turnips in. Sprinkle with the sugar. Fry briskly until the turnips caramelize to a golden colour. Keep stirring so as not to burn the sugar. Serve hot.

Lancashire Turnips and Carrots
This rough 'mash' of carrots and turnips is very English, very traditional – and substantial food.

SERVES 4

450 g (1 lb) turnips, peeled or scrubbed and roughly chopped

450 g (1 lb) carrots, peeled or scrubbed and roughly chopped

25 g (1 oz) butter or margarine

2 tablespoons flour

salt and freshly ground black pepper

slice of hot, buttered toast or a crisp salad, to serve

Cook the turnips and the carrots together in boiling water until soft. Drain, reserving the cooking liquid. Make a sauce by melting the butter or margarine over a low heat, stirring in the flour and gradually adding the cooking liquid, stirring all the time. Season, and simmer gently until the sauce thickens, about 6–8 minutes. Mash the vegetables roughly, season, and put them into a hot dish. Pour the hot sauce over the top and fold into the vegetables. Bake at 180°C/350°F/mark 4 for 25 minutes until bubbling. Serve with buttered toast or a crisp salad.

Jerusalem Artichokes

'Jerusalem' artichokes is a misnomer – they have nothing to do with the Holy Land. 'Jerusalem' is a corruption of *girasole*, or sunflower (the plant's generic name is *Helianthus tuberosus*). It is a stately, sculptural plant, ideal for siting along the edge of the vegetable garden.

Palestine Soup

A winter soup made with Jerusalem artichokes is a treat to look forward to as the cold weather arrives. Serve with warm granary rolls.

SERVES 4

900 g (2 lb) Jerusalem artichokes, washed and chopped

1 onion, peeled and chopped

25 g (1 oz) butter

salt and freshly ground black pepper

600 ml (1 pint) milk

600 ml (1 pint) Vegetable Stock (see page 154)

2 tablespoons single cream

Croûtons (see page 155), to serve

Place the artichokes and onion in a pan, cover with water and simmer until soft. Drain. Rub through a fine sieve, or purée in a blender or food processor. Stir in the butter, season well with salt and pepper, and mix in the milk and stock. Heat through and it is ready to serve. Swirl in the cream just before serving, and hand round Croûtons to sprinkle over the top.

Artichoke Fritters

Dipped into a light batter and cooked until golden and crisp in hot oil, these slices of artichoke are irresistible – wonderfully crisp on the outside, and runny inside. Serve either as a starter, sprinkled with parsley and a little sea salt, or as a side dish with poached fish or chicken.

SERVES 3–4

450 g (1 lb) Jerusalem artichokes, washed

flour

salt and freshly ground black pepper

1 recipe quantity Fritter Batter (see page 154)

vegetable oil for deep-frying

Parboil the artichokes in their skins for 10 minutes, or until tender but not mushy. Drain, and peel them when cooled. Slice them. Drop into well-seasoned flour, then coat in the batter. Deep-fry in very hot oil until crisp and golden all over. Drain on absorbent kitchen paper, and serve at once.

Artichoke and Leek Hot-Pot

A young English botanist, John Goodyear, writing in the early seventeenth century, was of the opinion that 'which way soever they be dressed and eaten they still cause a filthy loathsome stinking wind, thereby causing the belly to be pained and tormented'. But don't let him put you off: the artichoke – although admittedly windy – is a gastronomic vegetable, a delicacy, as this simple hot-pot illustrates. It tastes of the country – truly rural food – and is delicious served with crusty or wholemeal bread, as a light meal on its own, or as a side dish to accompany fish or meat.

SERVES 2–3

450 g (1 lb) Jerusalem artichokes, peeled and halved

2 medium leeks, washed, trimmed and cut into
   2.5 cm (1 in) lengths

salt and freshly ground black pepper

garam masala

900 ml (1½ pints) Vegetable Stock (see page 154)

2 tablespoons chopped fresh parsley

Pack the artichokes and leeks into a large casserole, seasoning a little as you go with salt, pepper and garam masala. Barely cover with the stock. Cover with a lid, and simmer very gently for about 12–15 minutes, until the vegetables are tender. Strain off the stock, season with more salt, pepper and garam masala, if necessary, and serve sprinkled with the chopped parsley.

Beetroot

Beetroot was developed by German gardeners in the Middle Ages, and it is a superb vegetable. Freshly dug baby beetroot are matchless – the smell of them while boiling is incomparable.

Beetroot Gratin

An old English cookery book describes how beetroot 'makes a colourful dish of "plain cooked vegetables" from the allotment', and although this is true, it is also to underrate it. Beetroot makes a wonderful dish in its own right, as this gratin demonstrates.

SERVES 3–4

6 medium beetroot, boiled and peeled

2 tablespoons grated Parmesan cheese

2 tablespoon grated Cheddar cheese

salt and freshly ground black pepper

5 tablespoons single cream

breadcrumbs

a little butter or margarine

Cut the beetroot into small dice. Sprinkle one-third of the cheeses over the bottom of a small gratin dish, and put half the beetroot on top, packed down tightly. Season, then repeat the layers, ending with a layer of cheese. Pour in enough cream just to cover, and scatter breadcrumbs over the top. Dot with butter or margarine. Bake in a preheated oven for 15 minutes at 190°C/375°F/mark 5.

Borsch

The most famous dish of the Russian culinary canon, borsch is indeed a major treat. Its rich colour and earthy flavours make it excellent warming winter food, yet borsch is also delicious served chilled – and always with that dollop of soured cream in the centre.

SERVES 4–6

450 g (1 lb) raw beetroot

1 small white cabbage, quartered

1.2 litres (2 pints) Vegetable Stock (see page 156)

2 tablespoons vinegar

2 potatoes, peeled and diced

salt and freshly ground black pepper

lemon juice to taste

sugar to taste

100 ml (3½ fl oz) soured cream

Peel the raw beetroot, and grate it coarsely. Blanch the white cabbage in boiling water for 3–4 minutes, then shred it finely. Put the cabbage into a large saucepan, and simmer in the stock until tender. In a separate pan, cook the grated beetroot in water with the vinegar until tender – about 10 minutes, then add, with the cooking liquid, to the cooked cabbage and stock. Add the diced potatoes, and season with salt and pepper. Add lemon juice and sugar to taste. Simmer for a further 25 minutes, or just until the flavours are well amalgamated. Purée in a blender or food processor, adjust the seasoning, and serve with a bowl of the soured cream to hand around.

Beetroot as a SIDE VEGETABLE

• Boil beetroot in their skins: wash them first, and peel after cooking in boiling water until tender – the length of cooking time required depends on the size.

• Roasted beetroot is delicious. Wash, peel, cut into chunks and drizzle with oil. Bake at 190°C/375°F/mark 5 for 40–45 minutes, or until tender, turning often. Serve with freshly ground black pepper .

• Sliced boiled beetroot is lovely with spinach, served in layers with a garnish of Croûtons (see page 155).

Carrots

Carrots have been popular in Britain since the end of the Middle Ages. They were, however, known to the Roman epicure Apicius, who gave recipes for fried carrots and carrots with parsnips. Later gardeners developed four main varieties: purple, yellow, white and orange. Nor was the root the only part used: in the time of Charles I ladies at Court wore carrot foliage in their hats!

Spiced Carrot Soup

This richly orange-coloured soup is a favourite standby for long periods of the year. It is thick and satisfying, the spiciness pleasing to the palate – and of course it is teeming with Vitamin A!

SERVES 2–3

450 g (1 lb) carrots, peeled or scrubbed

1–2 teaspoons garam masala paste

600 ml (1 pint) Vegetable Stock (see page 154)

cream or yoghurt to taste

sea salt

thin toast or pitta bread, to serve

Simmer the carrots in a pan of water until very well cooked. Blend to a purée with the garam masala paste and stock in a blender or food processor. Thin out to the desired consistency, if necessary, with a little water, and add some cream or yoghurt to taste. Heat through, but do not boil. Season to taste with a little sea salt, and serve immediately with thin toast or pitta bread.

Glazed Carrots

In medieval times vegetables were called 'wortes', and usually boiled to death with a flank of fairly tough meat. How times have changed: these glazed carrots have subtlety and a light touch.

SERVES 3–4

325 g (12 oz) carrots, peeled or scrubbed

1 tablespoon butter or margarine

2 tablespoons sugar

salt

Slice the carrots diagonally. Cover with water in a saucepan, add the butter or margarine, sugar and a pinch of salt. Boil steadily until almost cooked, then turn up the heat to cook vigorously, in order to reduce the liquid down to a shiny glaze. Be careful not to overdo it or else the glaze will caramelize.

Left: *Glazed carrots*

Gratin of Carrots *This completely unpretentious dish is delicate and satisfying, and an appetizing contrast of creamy and crisp textures.*

SERVES 3–4

450 g (1 lb) carrots, peeled or scrubbed, thickly sliced and cooked

1 recipe quantity Béchamel Sauce (see page 154)

2 tablespoons single cream

salt and freshly ground black pepper

40 g (1½ oz) cheese, grated

40 g (1½ oz) breadcrumbs

melted butter or margarine

Put the cooked carrots into the Béchamel Sauce, and stir in the cream. Season to taste, then put in an oven-proof dish. Top with the grated cheese mixed with the breadcrumbs. Dribble a little melted butter or margarine over the top, and brown in a preheated oven at 190°C/375°F/mark 5 for 10 minutes.

Best Carrot Cake *'Sowe Carrets in your Gardens, and humbly praise God for them, as for a singular and great blessing,' says Richard Gardiner in his* Profitable Instructions for the Manuring, Sowing and Planting of Kitchen gardens *of 1599. A blessing indeed: where would we be without carrot cake? This one is brilliant, the best recipe I know. It freezes well.*

SERVES 6

100 g (4 oz) margarine

175 g (6 oz) sugar

3 eggs

225 g (8 oz) flour

1 teaspoon bicarbonate of soda

2 teaspoons cinnamon

450 g (1 lb) carrots, peeled or scrubbed and finely grated

75 g (3 oz) raisins or sultanas

40 g (1½ oz) chopped nuts, such as walnuts or pecan (optional)

Cream the margarine with the sugar, then beat in the eggs alternately with half of the flour, sifted with the bicarbonate of soda and the cinnamon. Stir in the carrots, and fold in the rest of the flour. Finally, stir in the raisins or sultanas, and the nuts, if using. Place in a greased 20 cm (8 in) cake tin and bake in a preheated oven at 180°C/350°F/mark 4 for 40–45 minutes, until just set – it wants to be still a little moist in the centre; the cooking time varies according to the water content of the carrots. Cool a little in the tin, then turn on to a wire rack, and leave until cold.

Celeriac
Although introduced into Britain in the 1720s, celeriac is only just coming into its own and making its mark on the British culinary consciousness. It has a beautiful flavour, and is a valuable and interesting winter vegetable. It discolours when cut, so dip it into acidulated water (2 tablespoons lemon juice or 1 tablespoon vinegar, to 1.2 litres/2 pints water).

Celeriac Rémoulade
This salad, best served as an hors d'oeuvre, is of French inspira

SERVES 4

1 medium celeriac root, peeled

1 recipe quantity Mayonnaise (see page 122)

1–2 tablespoons Dijon mustard to taste

chopped fresh parsley, to garnish

Cut the peeled celeriac into fine julienne strips. Mix the Mayonnaise with the mustard, check for flavour, and then mix thoroughly with the celeriac. Garnish with chopped parsley.

Celeriac Gratin
Slices of cooked celeriac in a cheese or tomato sauce, and topped with a crust of breadcrumbs and cheese, make a delightful side dish, or a perfect meal for vegetarians, served with crusty bread and a winter salad

SERVES 2–3

1 small-medium celeriac root, peeled

25 g (1 oz) Parmesan cheese, grated

25–40 g (1–1½ oz) butter or margarine

Béchamel Sauce (see page 154) or Fresh Tomato Sauce (see page 102)

40 g (1½ oz) Cheddar cheese, grated

50 g (2 oz) fresh granary breadcrumbs

Cut the celeriac into slices, and cook in boiling water until tender. Arrange in a buttered gratin dish, scattering each layer with the grated Parmesan and knobs of butter or margarine. Cover with the sauce of your choice. Mix the grated Cheddar with the breadcrumbs, and sprinkle over the top. Dot with little pieces of the remaining butter or margarine, and bake in a preheated oven at 180°C/350°F/mark 4 for 20 minutes, until nicely browned.

Leeks
The strong Welsh connection with the leek is its primary association for many people. In AD 640 the Welsh fought a successful battle against the Saxons, and according to legend stuck leeks in their hats to distinguish themselves from the enemy.

Leeks disappeared from the tables of the gentry in the sixteenth and seventeenth centuries, and have only relatively recently made their return to popularity. Leeks are best eaten fairly young, before they grow too thick, and they don't improve with long cooking.

Crème Vichyssoise
In spite of its French name this is an American soup, invented in New York and first served at the Ritz Carlton in 1917. It is stunning: an unforgettable pale green colour, with delicate, fine flavours. Serve chilled, sprinkled with chives.

SERVES 4–6

6 leeks, washed, trimmed and finely sliced

50 g (2 oz) unsalted butter

5 medium potatoes, peeled and finely sliced

1.5 litres (2½ pints) Vegetable Stock (see page 154)

salt

175 ml (6 fl oz) thick cream or *crème fraîche*

chopped fresh chives, to garnish

Soften the leeks in the butter over a gentle heat for 5–6 minutes. Add the potatoes, and cook for a further 5 minutes, stirring. Add the stock and salt to taste, and simmer gently for 30–40 minutes, covered. Purée in a blender or food processor until very smooth. Cool.

When the soup is cold, stir in the cream or *crème fraîche*, and then chill thoroughly. Serve sprinkled with chopped fresh chives.

Leekie Pie
Dorothy Hartley writes of leeks in Food in England, *'it is a mistake to serve these delicate vegetables with thick sauce; the liquor and butter together in the dish should be sufficient.' She is right; braised in milk and/or butter until just tender, they are superb, either as a side dish or as here in an old-fashioned pie.*

SERVES 4

1½ recipe quantities Shortcrust Pastry (see page 150)

1.25 kg (2½ lb) thin leeks, washed, trimmed and
  thinly sliced

40 g (1½ oz) butter or margarine

salt and freshly ground black pepper

Roll out two-thirds of the pastry, and use to line a greased deep 22 cm (9 in) pie dish. Soften the leeks slightly by sweating them in the butter or margarine, in a covered pan, for 10 minutes, stirring occasionally. Pack them into the pie dish, and season with salt and pepper. Roll out the remaining pastry to form a lid, and use to cover the pie. Seal the edges well. Make a slit in the top of the pie. Bake in a preheated oven at 190°C/375°F/mark 5 for 40–50 minutes, until the crust is a fine crisp brown. Serve hot or warm.

Flamiche
The Victorians decreed that leeks 'tainted the breath', and deemed them peasant food. But leeks are a fine winter vegetable, which lend themselves to gastronomic dishes. This flamiche, *or open tart, is a fine example of peasant food of distinction.*

SERVES 3–4

Dough:

150 g (5 oz) plain flour, plus extra for kneading

40 g (1½ oz) butter or margarine, cut into small
  pieces

salt

15 g (½ oz) active dried yeast, dissolved in
  2 tablespoons warm water

1 egg, beaten

Filling:

1.5 kg (3 lb) leeks, washed

50 g (2 oz) butter or margarine

3 egg yolks

150 ml (¼ pint) *crème fraîche*

salt and freshly ground black pepper

To make the dough, sift the flour, and rub in the pieces of butter or margarine. Add a pinch of salt. Make a well in the centre, and put in the yeast mixture and the beaten egg. Mix, and knead until smooth. Add a little water if necessary. Roll into a ball, and make a cross-cut on the top. Place in a bowl, and leave in a warm place, covered with a cloth, to rise for 2 hours.

About 30 minutes before the dough is ready, start to prepare the filling. Chop the white part of the leeks (reserving the green part for soup or stock), and stew in the butter or margarine until cooked to a pulp.

When the dough is ready, sprinkle with flour and knock it back. Knead, and press into a 20 cm (8 in) tart tin with your knuckles. Spread the leeks on top. Beat the egg yolks with the *crème fraîche*, and season with salt and pepper. Pour over the leeks. Bake at 200°C/400°F/mark 6 for 20 minutes, then at 180°C/350°F/mark 4 for a further 20 minutes. Serve hot or warm.

Onions

The onion, chief of the *Allium* family of which garlic, too, is a member, is older than recorded history. So venerated was it in ancient Egypt that the priests forbade the people to eat it. An onion was placed in the hands of mummies to help their journey to the underworld, as it would ward off evil and give them protection.

Tarte à l'Oignon

This tart is country cooking at its best – simple, and with that sublimely sweet flavour of melted onions.

SERVES 6–8

1 recipe quantity Shortcrust Pastry (see page 150)

700 g (1½ lb) onions, peeled and thinly sliced

40 g (1½ oz) butter or margarine

2 eggs, beaten

50 g (2 oz) Gruyère cheese, grated

salt, freshly ground black pepper and nutmeg

Roll out the pastry, and use to line a greased 22 cm (9 in) tart tin. Stew the onions in the butter or margarine for 30 minutes, with the pan covered, stirring occasionally and making sure that they don't brown. Remove from the heat and stir in the beaten eggs. Fold in the grated Gruyère. Season with salt, pepper and nutmeg. Pour into the pastry shell, and bake at 180°C/350°F/mark 4 for 20–30 minutes, until set. Serve warm or cold.

Pickled ONIONS

Bread-and-cheese-and-pickled-onions was traditional country food for centuries, carried in a bag or pocket to the fields for the noonday meal. Pickled onions were made in vast quantities by rural folk, using small onions especially grown for the purpose.

Pick the largest of the onions off the top of the stalk. Peel them, and put into 10 per cent Brine (see page 149) for 3 days. Remove and drain them, then rinse and pack into jars. Pour cold Spiced Vinegar (see page 149) over them. Cover and seal, then leave for 6 months before using.

To make decorative jars for presents, arrange the onions in the jars with red chillies and green capers. You can also tint the vinegar golden by boiling the papery outer skins of onion in it.

Right: *Pickled onions*

Spring Onion TANSY

The 'tansy' is a cross between scrambled eggs and an omelette, cooked with onion tops or spring onions. A delightful, simple dish for a light supper, served with new potatoes and a tossed salad. I can't improve on the wording of this old country recipe:

Take holsters [bolted onions] in spring, chop them finely and fry in bacon fat. When they are soft drain off any fat, and pour on enough beaten egg to cover, and pepper and salt to chase them around – until blended – and then 'leave 'em be' till set, 'not let them boil, mind, or the egg will be all a whey, just set it nicely.' Turn on to a hot plate, and it is excellent.

I made this recipe for two people using 3 spring onions, 3 eggs and 15 g (½ oz) margarine. We ate it for lunch with fresh granary bread and a tossed salad, and it was a feast.

Soubise

Soubise is a purée of onions, which have been cooked very slowly and gently until they are soft and sweet and have lost their pungency, a technique which is the basis of soupe à l'oignon gratinée, *one of France's great peasant dishes. Soubise is a delectable sauce, wonderful with chicken and new potatoes, or over soft-boiled eggs.*

MAKES 450 ML (¾ PINT)

225 g (8 oz) onions, peeled and very thinly sliced

40 g (1½ oz) butter or margarine

1 tablespoon flour, sifted

salt, freshly ground black pepper and nutmeg

150 ml (¼ pint) warm milk or stock

single cream (optional)

Soften the sliced onions in the butter or margarine in a pan over a gentle heat, covered with a lid, for about 12–15 minutes, until pale yellow in colour but not browned. Stir from time to time. When they have all but melted, stir in the flour, and season to taste with salt, pepper and a little nutmeg. Add the milk or stock, and simmer very gently for 15 minutes.

Sieve or blend so that the sauce is quite smooth. Thin out, if necessary, with single cream, and check the seasoning.

Onionskin EGGS

Cut the outer skin carefully from larger onions, and wrap it around eggs with a wet cloth. Tie securely. Boil the eggs until they are hard. Cool in cold water, then remove the cloth and onionskin, and dry. You can then polish them with grease and you will have a beautifully shiny, mottled, striped or marbled golden-brown egg.

Celery Celery never played much of a role in English cookery until after the 1880s. It has to be blanched up, that is, grown in trenches, but you are well rewarded if you do grow your own – both taste and texture are a revelation.

Celery and Cheese Soup *Do use the leaves as well as the stalks when you are making celery soup – they add immensely to the flavour. This soup is inimitable, served on a very cold day for lunch with crusty bread and butter. If you like blue cheese, you can try making it with Danish Blue or Stilton.*

SERVES 4

1 medium head of celery, trimmed and chopped

2 medium onions, peeled and chopped

50 g (2 oz) butter or margarine

25 g (1 oz) plain flour

1.2 litres (2 pints) Vegetable Stock (see page 154)

50 g (2 oz) Gruyère or Cheddar cheese, grated

salt and freshly ground black pepper

2 tablespoons chopped fresh parsley or dill

triangles of fried bread or fingers of toast, to serve

Cook the chopped vegetables in the butter or margarine over a gentle heat, covered, for 10 minutes until soft but not brown. Stir in the flour, then add the stock slowly, stirring until the mixture becomes smooth and thick. Cover, and simmer for 40 minutes, until the celery is very tender.

Purée in a blender or food processor. Return to the heat, and add the grated cheese. Heat gently until the cheese melts. Check the seasoning, and stir in the herbs. Serve with triangles of fried bread, or fingers of toast.

Winter SALADS

John Evelyn, the eighteenth-century diarist, called celery 'the grace of the whole board', meaning when served with cheese, and how right he was. Fresh, crisp, raw celery is one of the winter's best things, and perfect in salads. Use the 'hearts', too, for their unique flavour and texture. Here are a few salad ideas:

• chopped celery with Jerusalem artichokes (chopped raw), and mustard-and-cress

• Waldorf salad: chopped celery, chopped apple and chopped walnuts in mayonnaise

• chopped celery, chopped apple and cubes of Gruyère cheese in mayonnaise

• celery, tomatoes, beetroot and chopped hazelnuts in mayonnaise

• chopped celery, potatoes and beetroot in mayonnaise

A s p a r a g u s *I revere the memory of Mr F as an estimable man and most indulgent husband, only necessary to mention Asparagus and it appears ... it was not ecstasy but it was comfort.*

Flora Finching in *Little Dorrit*, Charles Dickens, 1857

Asparagus Soup *An elegant and delicate summer soup, you can serve this either hot, with Croûtons (see page 155), or chilled with Melba Toast (see page 155). It is one of the delights of high summer.*

SERVES 4

24 medium stalks asparagus, washed and woody part
   of stems removed

1 shallot, peeled and finely chopped

900 ml (1½ pints) Vegetable Stock (see page 154)

salt and freshly ground black pepper

25 g (1 oz) butter

25 g (1 oz) flour

300 ml (½ pint) cream

Cut the asparagus stems into 2.5 cm (1 in) lengths, saving eight tips for garnish. Simmer the shallot with the asparagus in the stock, covered, for about 20 minutes. Meanwhile, steam the reserved tips until just tender, and keep warm on one side.

Process the stock with the cooked shallot and asparagus in a blender or food processor until smooth, and pass through a sieve, if necessary, if there are stringy bits still in the purée. Heat through, and season to taste.

Work the butter and the flour to a smooth paste, divide into small pieces and whisk, off the heat, into the soup. Heat gently, stirring constantly, until thickened and well blended. Serve hot or chilled. Swirl the cream into each portion as you serve up, adding two of the reserved tips to each bowl.

To steam ASPARAGUS

Trim the woody ends off the asparagus stems, wash, then sort into bundles of even size, and tie up with string. Cook them upright in a tall saucepan so that only the thick stems stand in boiling water, and the delicate heads are just steamed. When ready, they should be just tender, but still have some 'bite'; this will take 8–10 minutes, depending on the thickness of the stems. Lift out carefully and lay flat on a warmed plate before removing the string.

Asparagus Tart
A classic quiche made with freshly gathered home-grown asparagus – and, if possible, with your own eggs – is a gastronomic experience, a far cry from mass-produced freezer food, or even a home-made tart made with commercially grown asparagus. You will really taste the difference!

SERVES 4

1 recipe quantity Shortcrust Pastry (see page 150)

1 tablespoon butter or margarine

2 tablespoons grated onion or shallot

1 tablespoon chopped fresh tarragon or parsley

2 eggs

150 ml (¼ pint) single cream

salt and freshly ground black pepper

50 g (2 oz) Gruyère cheese, diced (optional)

8–10 fresh asparagus spears, steamed (see page 84)

Roll out the pastry thinly, and use to line a 22 cm (9 in) flan tin.

Melt the butter or margarine, and cook the grated onion or shallot in it until soft, about 3–4 minutes. Remove from the heat, and stir in the tarragon or parsley. Beat in the eggs with the cream, and season well. If you want a richer dish, add the diced Gruyère cheese at this point.

Arrange the cooked asparagus spears on the bottom of the pastry case, pour the egg and cream mixture over the top, and bake in a preheated oven at 180°C/350°F/mark 4 for 40 minutes. Cool a little on a wire rack, and serve warm.

Asparagus Frittata
Some gardeners like to grow asparagus as much for its decorative fern in late summer and autumn, as for its succulent stems. Whether you choose to grow it in the herbaceous border or in the vegetable garden, this frittata – a Mediterranean omelette – is an easy way of enjoying your crop.

SERVES 2–3

450 g (1 lb) asparagus, washed and woody part of
   stems removed

2 tablespoons good olive oil

4 eggs

4 tablespoons grated Pecorino or Parmesan cheese

salt and freshly ground black pepper

Steam the asparagus until just tender (see page 84). Cut into 2.5 cm (1 in) lengths. Heat half of the olive oil in a heavy pan, and toss the asparagus in it over a moderate heat for 2 minutes. Remove from the pan and drain.

Beat the eggs, and fold in the cheese. Season to taste. Add the asparagus, and mix well. Add the remaining oil to the pan, heat gently, then pour in the egg mixture. Cook over a moderate heat until the bottom is nicely browned. Then slide the frittata on to a plate, and toss back into the pan so that the uncooked side is on the bottom of the pan. Cook until the underside is golden, and serve immediately.

Lettuces

Lettuces are mentioned in a fifteenth-century book on gardening, at which time they were more likely to be eaten cooked along with other 'pot herbs', rather than in salads. They make a very appetizing cooked vegetable, lightly braised – in stuffed pancakes, for example, or in soup – in both cases combined with peas: the combination is legendary. You can also add shredded lettuce to a stir-fry.

A fair herb, that men call lettuce.

S. England Legends, Anon, 1290

The Elizabethans began to eat lettuce raw, and salad came into high fashion in the sixteenth century. Was this perhaps because – they claimed – lettuce was an aphrodisiac? The Romans, on the other hand, maintained that the lettuce upheld morals, and engendered temperance and chastity. The Greeks, however, valued it for its soporific qualities, and right through to the twentieth century this has been its folklore. In *Food In England* (1954) Dorothy Hartley writes:

... the expressed juice of the lettuce is one of the oldest soporifics. The juice was dried on plates, and afterwards bound into white cakes. It was given to patients before and after surgical operations in conjunction with poppy seeds.

John Evelyn, writing in the seventeenth century, wrote that the lettuce 'ever was and still continues the principal foundation of the universal Tribe of Salads: which is to cool and refresh'. In his *Acetaria* (1699) he developed his theory of good salad-making:

In the composure of a salad every plant should come in to bear its part, without being overpowered by some herb of a stronger taste ... but fall into their places, like the notes in music, in which there should be nothing harsh or grating.

This advice can hardly be improved upon. Nowadays there are many salad vegetables to choose from. Varieties of lettuce alone include Iceberg, Cos, Webb's Wonder, Cabbage lettuce, Oak Leaf, Endive (Frisée), Butternut, Little Gem and Lollo Rosso, to name but some.

Supplemented with a selection of wonderful crisp chicory, celery, cucumber, spring onions, as well as other leaves and fresh herbs, we are spoiled for choice. So choose your ingredients, making sure they are fresh and clean, and after washing shake them dry in a spinner or clean towel.

Dress them in a good dressing, using the best quality olive oil possible, ideally that golden-green olive oil of the first pressing – 'Smooth, light and pleasant upon the tongue' (John Evelyn again). Mix the oil with the best wine or herb vinegar, some sea salt and top quality mustard, of which Dijon takes my prize. Some people like to put a pinch of sugar into a dressing, too, and sometimes some crushed garlic. But don't be heavy handed on either: keep the vinaigrette delicate, and adjust according to your taste (see basic Vinaigrette recipe on page 155).

Lambs' Lettuce and Beetroot Salad *Lambs' lettuce was given this name by John Gerard in his* Herbal *of 1597. One country name for it is corn salad* – mache *in French.*

SERVES 4

150 g (5 oz) lambs' lettuce, washed

½ recipe quantity Vinaigrette (see page 155)

1 large beetroot, boiled and peeled

1 small apple, peeled and grated

1 hard-boiled egg, finely chopped

Toss the lambs' lettuce with the Vinaigrette. Cut the beetroot into thin strips, then toss into the salad with the grated apple. Scatter the finely chopped egg over the top, and serve.

Lambs' Lettuce and Baby Spinach Salad *Lambs' lettuce is a tender, tasty addition to the summer salad bowl, and this is a salad of some elegance.*

SERVES 4

100 g (4 oz) each lambs' lettuce and baby spinach
  leaves, washed

a few fresh sorrel leaves, torn

1 tablespoon chopped fresh herbs

½ recipe quantity Vinaigrette (see page 155)

50 g (2 oz) Gruyère cheese, finely diced

Tear any large lambs' lettuce and baby spinach leaves into smaller pieces and mix together with the herbs. Toss in the Vinaigrette. Add the diced cheese and toss again.

Salade des Vignerons
A rustic recipe from France, this unusual starter is a mixture of salad leaves with a hot dressing poured over it, tossed and served immediately. The flavour of the lambs' lettuce is wonderful with the touch of beetroot and the vinegary dressing.

75 g (3 oz) lambs' lettuce, washed

½ medium endive (frisée lettuce), washed

a few young dandelion leaves, blanched

1 medium beetroot, boiled and peeled, and cut

  into strips

salt and freshly ground black pepper

5 tablespoons olive oil

3 tablespoons white wine vinegar

Dry the salad leaves well, and place in a salad bowl. Put the beetroot in the centre, and season with salt and pepper.

Heat the olive oil until just smoking, and pour over the salad. Quickly add the white wine vinegar to the hot pan, sizzle it, and when it foams pour quickly over the salad. Toss and serve the salad immediately.

Other SALAD LEAVES
Landcress and rocket grow very easily in the vegetable patch. Both have a long summer season, and are excellent salad leaves. Rocket has a particularly distinctive peppery taste.

Watercress
There is a well-known old-wives' tale claiming that watercress purifies the blood, and so in the old days it was recommended as a spring salad after the long grey winter. It is indeed a valuable salad leaf, rich in iron, crisp and with a peppery bite to its flavour. Its deep green turns to a delicate bronze as the leaf matures, and always looks beautiful with a mixture of other greens in the salad bowl.

Watercress is the perfect accompaniment to the cheese board – it does for Caerphilly and Double Gloucester what celery does for Stilton. Don't chill watercress, however – it goes limp. Just wash it, and keep in a bowl of cold water until ready to use.

Sorrel
Raw, the leaves of sorrel are an excellent thirst-quencher. 'The mower gladly chews it down,' writes John Clare in the *Shepherd's Calendar* (1827), 'and slakes his thirst as best he may.'

Sorrel Soup
Sorrel, with its lemony flavour and sharp bite, can be used in the same way as spinach in soufflés and quiches, and is delicious added to a herb omelette. Use the young raw leaves in salads and sandwiches. Here it makes a lively and refreshing soup for hot weather. It is delicious served with warm granary rolls.

SERVES 4

½ onion, peeled and finely sliced

40 g (1½ oz) butter or margarine

2 medium potatoes, peeled and diced

1.2 litres (2 pints) Vegetable Stock (see page 156)

salt, freshly ground black pepper and nutmeg

2 handfuls of fresh sorrel leaves, washed and stalks removed

3–4 tablespoons *crème fraîche*

Croûtons (see page 155), to serve

Cook the sliced onion in the butter or margarine in a saucepan until soft. Add the diced potatoes, and stir until coated. The pour in the stock, season, and simmer over a gentle heat until the potatoes are soft – about 12–15 minutes.

Remove the central ribs from the sorrel leaves, and place in a blender or food processor. Pour the hot soup base over, and blend until smooth (do this with a little of the soup base at a time). Return to the clean pan, reheat and check the seasoning. Serve with a swirl of crème fraîche in each bowl, and scatter the top with Croûtons before handing around.

You can make a green soup of sorrel, lettuce and watercress in the same way.

Simple SORREL SAUCE

This sauce is simplicity itself to make, and freezes well. Its lemony sharpness gives a pleasing balance to grilled fish or chicken, and is excellent with poached eggs,

Remove the stalks from the sorrel leaves, and wash them. Put into a saucepan, without any added water, with a knob of margarine or butter, and cook gently until the sorrel becomes a soft mass. Chop finely, and remove any stringy bits. Thin out with a little stock and/or cream, and it is ready to serve.

Spinach The first record of spinach comes from China, although it was the

Persians who developed its cultivation in the sixth century. It travelled via North Africa to Spain,

What a world of gammon and spinnage it is, though, ain't it!

David Copperfield, Charles Dickens, 1850

where it was being grown by the eleventh century. Its great taste and nutritional richness (lots of iron and vitamins) have helped it to remain a firm favourite with the gardener and cook alike.

Spinach Roulade *The sight of a roulade can be so impressive as to be daunting. But with careful handling and precise timing, it tuns out easily and is a wonderful meal served with a salad such as the Cottage Garden Salad on page 57.*

SERVES 4

6 spring onions, trimmed and finely chopped

225 g (8 oz) cottage cheese, drained

½ recipe quantity Béchamel Sauce (see page 154)

salt, freshly ground black pepper and nutmeg

225 g (8 oz) cooked fresh spinach, finely chopped

4 eggs, separated

1 tablespoon grated Gruyère cheese

1 tablespoon grated Parmesan cheese

1 recipe quantity Fresh Tomato Sauce (see page 102), to serve

Fold the chopped spring onions into the cottage cheese with 4 tablespoons of the Béchamel Sauce. Cook gently for 3 minutes, and season to taste with salt, pepper and nutmeg. Set on one side.

Blend the spinach in a blender or food processor with the rest of the Béchamel Sauce and the egg yolks. Season to taste, and stir in the grated cheeses. Whisk the egg whites until stiff, and gently fold in. Line a 33 x 22 cm (13 x 9 in) Swiss roll tin with foil and grease it well. Spread the spinach mixture over it evenly, and bake in a preheated oven at 190°C/375°F/mark 5 for 15 minutes.

Remove from the oven, put a clean cloth over the top, and invert on to a flat surface. Leave for 5 minutes, then lift off the tin and remove the foil.

Spread with the cottage cheese mixture, leaving a margin around the edges. Ease carefully into a roll, using the cloth to lift it. Then flip the roulade on to a warm serving dish so that it sits with the join underneath. Serve with the Fresh Tomato Sauce.

Oeufs Florentines *The classic way of using spinach as a bed for lightly poached eggs.*

SERVES 2

325 g (12 oz) fresh spinach, cooked and drained

4 poached eggs

½ recipe quantity Béchamel Sauce (see page 154)

50 g (2 oz) Cheddar cheese, grated

2 tablespoons grated Parmesan cheese

Make a bed of the still warm spinach in the bottom of a gratin dish, or in two individual cocotte dishes. Arrange the lightly poached eggs on top.

Heat the Béchamel Sauce gently, and stir in the Cheddar cheese until melted. Coat the eggs and spinach with the sauce, and sprinkle with the grated Parmesan cheese. Put under a hot grill for a minute or so, until the top browns and the dish bubbles. Serve immediately.

Cabbage The cabbage has an ancient history, having been eaten in Britain by the ancient Celts and Romans. In his *Satires* Juvenal wrote 'that cabbage hashed up again and again proves the death of the wretched teachers', and the poor cabbage has never lived down its links with institutional food, invariably boiled to extinction. There are, however, some refined ways of cooking cabbage.

Red Cabbage with Apple *Casseroled red cabbage, cooked very slowly in the oven with stock and apples, and perhaps a little red wine, makes robust food for a hearty supper on a cold winter's night. It goes extremely well with game birds and mashed potatoes.*

SERVES 6

1 small red cabbage, washed and sliced

2–3 Cox apples, cored and sliced

salt and freshly ground black pepper

600 ml (1 pint) Vegetable Stock (see page 156)

2–3 tablespoons red wine (optional)

Layer the red cabbage with the apples in an ovenproof casserole, seasoning as you go. Cover with stock, and add a little red wine if you like. Cover the casserole with foil and also a lid, and cook 2 hours in a preheated oven at 170°C/325°F/mark 3 for 1½–2 hours, turning with a wooden spoon halfway through the time. You can also layer 225 g (8 oz) chestnuts (dried ones do well) with the cabbage and apple, for a fuller, richer dish.

Cabbage SALADS

Fourteenth-century physicians recommended those with weak heads for drink to chew cabbage leaves. So presumably all these salads would have a similar preventive effect! In any case, crisp white cabbage makes an excellent salad ingredient for the winter, and there are endless variations that you can experiment with, using nuts and seeds and fruit as well as other vegetables, either raw or lightly cooked. Here are a few suggestions:

• Shredded cabbage with grated horseradish, chopped onion and radishes, in Vinaigrette (see page 155)

• Finely shredded cabbage with grated cheese, grated carrot, raisins and chopped apple, in a coleslaw dressing (equal quantities of Mayonnaise [see page 122], yoghurt and lemon juice, seasoned with salt and pepper)

• Shredded cabbage with chopped celery, sliced red peppers and raw onion rings, in Vinaigrette (see page 155)

• Shredded cabbage with chopped dried apricots that have been soaked in orange juice, chopped walnuts and orange segments, in Mayonnaise (see page 122) or Vinaigrette (see page 155)

• Shredded cabbage with very finely sliced raw Brussels sprouts and turnips

Bubble and Squeak

The first Savoy cabbages arrived from Holland in the 1570s: 'Tis scarce 100 years since we had Cabbages out of Holland, Sir Arthur Ashley, of Wilburg St Giles, in Dorsetshire, being the first who planted them in England,' says the Gardener's Book *of 1699. I have a hunch that Bubble and Squeak is probably about as old, so firmly entrenched is it in the traditions of English cookery,*

YOU WILL NEED: • cooked potatoes • cooked cabbage, chopped • onion, chopped • dripping or margarine • salt and freshly ground black pepper

Put the potatoes through a ricer, or mash them well. Mix thoroughly with the chopped cabbage. Cook the onion in margarine or dripping and, when soft and lightly browned, press in the cabbage and potato mixture evenly. Sprinkle with salt and pepper. Cook gently. When well crusted and deep brown on the underside – this will take about 10–15 minutes – turn and brown the other side. Turn out on to a heated dish.

This makes a perfect supper dish by the fireside in winter, served with fried eggs and some warm, crusty home-made bread.

Brussels Sprouts

It is thought that Brussels sprouts originated in the thriving market gardens of the Low Countries during the Middle Ages. They are miniature cabbages in bud form, growing up the stem of a plant derived from the wild cabbage, and have a strong distinctive flavour. Sprouts have long been popular in winter cookery – their season lasts from September to April – and they are traditionally an integral part of Christmas dinner. They quick-freeze very well, retaining their colour, taste and texture.

Pan-Fried Brussels Sprouts

Escoffier's version of this goes: 'Throw them into an omelette pan containing some very hot butter and toss them in until they are nicely frizzled.' It is a brilliant idea: this otherwise fairly mundane vegetable is vastly improved by this way of cooking.

Brussels sprouts, trimmed and washed	butter or margarine
salt and freshly ground black pepper	

Cook the sprouts in boiling salted water, then drain well. Melt a large knob of butter or margarine in a pan until it is very hot, put in the sprouts and toss over a brisk heat for 3–4 minutes, shaking the pan. Season with lots of black pepper.

As a variation, you can chop the sprouts up first, stew them until well softened, and then combine with as much cream as you like.

Purée of BRUSSELS SPROUTS

This is nothing less than epicurean, a revelation. It seems inconceivable that this dish is produced from the ordinary little Brussels sprout.

Cook sprouts in as little water as possible, for as short a time as possible, so they are cooked through but still slightly crunchy. Put into a blender or food processor with a little cooking liquid and some cream. Whizz to a wonderful green purée, season to taste with salt, freshly ground black pepper and nutmeg and thin out with more cream or cooking liquid as necessary.

This is delicious served with an Omelette or Kookoo (see page 123).

Globe Artichokes
The globe artichoke – 'noble thistle' according to John Evelyn – looks sculptural and dignified in the vegetable patch. It has a fine, delicate flavour, and was once regarded as an aphrodisiac, which is probably the reason why it featured quite frequently in Renaissance feasts!

Stuffed Artichokes
For a party piece, serve globe artichokes like this, with a delectable stuffing of lightly spiced, minced mushrooms, set on a bed of lightly dressed salad leaves.

SERVES 2

2 large globe artichokes

225 g (8 oz) button mushrooms, wiped

3 spring onions, trimmed and finely sliced

1 teaspoon mild curry paste

squeeze of lemon juice

3–4 tablespoons Mayonnaise (see page 122)

mixed salad leaves

Vinaigrette (see page 155)

Trim the stems off the artichokes, cutting them flush with the bottom. Remove the tough outer leaves, and trim the sharp pointed tips off the remaining leaves. Cook the artichokes in boiling water, covered, for 30–40 minutes, until tender. Drain and cool. When cool enough to handle, carefully pull back the leaves of each artichoke to expose the fibrous inner centre – the 'choke'. Carefully scrape away the choke, and discard.

Put the mushrooms into a blender or food processor, and process until they are finely minced. Steam with the sliced spring onions in the microwave, or in a steamer. Cool, then drain well. Mix in the curry paste, lemon juice and Mayonnaise, and pile into the centre of the dechoked artichokes.

To serve, arrange each stuffed artichoke decoratively on a bed of mixed salad leaves, which have been lightly dressed in Vinaigrette. Dip each leaf into the mushroom filling as you eat, and finish off any remaining filling with the tender artichoke heart.

Left: *Stuffed artichokes*

Broccoli Broccoli is, to my taste, as indeed to many others, the king of the *Brassica* family. Its wonderful flavour is good hot or cold, and it goes well with numerous other ingredients, making it a versatile and welcome addition to the vegetable patch.

Broccoli and Pasta Gratin *This pasta gratin is a huge favourite with my family and has been for many years.*

SERVES 4

325 g (12 oz) pasta shapes, such as twists, shells, bows or quills

450 g (1 lb) broccoli spears

salt, freshly ground black pepper and nutmeg

1½ recipe quantities Béchamel Sauce (see page 154)

2 teaspoons chopped tarragon or 1 teaspoon dried

4 tablespoons white wine

6 tablespoons *crème fraîche*

2 tablespoons grated Parmesan cheese

50 g (2 oz) breadcrumbs

butter or margarine

Cook the pasta and broccoli separately in boiling salted water until they are tender but still have 'bite'. Put the cooked pasta in the bottom of a buttered gratin dish. Cover with the broccoli. Heat the Béchamel Sauce gently, and add the tarragon, white wine, *crème fraîche* and seasoning to taste. Stir in the cheese. Pour this sauce over the pasta and broccoli and sprinkle with the breadcrumbs. Dot with butter or margarine, and bake in a pre-heated oven at 190°C/375°F/mark 5 for 25 minutes, until it bubbles at the edges and is golden brown on top.

Broccoli Soup *A simple soup, rather more like a thick purée, of broccoli and stock makes a wonderful light lunch at almost any time of the year, eaten with wholemeal pitta bread. The soup freezes very well, so make lots of it if you ever have a glut of broccoli.*

SERVES 2–3

900 g (2 lb) broccoli, cooked until tender

900 ml (1½ pints) Vegetable Stock (see page 154)

salt, freshly ground black pepper and nutmeg

yoghurt, to serve (optional)

Put the cooked broccoli into a blender or food processor with the stock, and blend to a smooth purée. Heat through, and season to taste with salt, pepper and nutmeg. Serve the soup hot with a swirl of yoghurt in the centre if you like.

Cauliflower 'Coleflower' means 'cabbage flower'. It was first

cultivated in medieval times – records show that cauliflowers were being grown in Europe in the thirteenth century. Closely related to calabrese and broccoli – officially slow-maturing winter cauliflowers – summer and autumn cauliflowers are now widely grown. They are immensely popular for their delicate flavour, and are a versatile vegetable. You can eat cauliflower raw in salads, or cooked with any variety of sauces, or frittered, and it is famously good in pickles.

Cauliflower Soup *'Cauliflower juice in vinegar' was, so they claimed in medieval times, a cure for a hangover. It sounds so awful that I would advise avoiding the hangover, and drinking this soup instead. It makes a wonderful lunchtime warmer throughout the winter.*

SERVES 2–3

1 medium cauliflower

900 ml (1½ pints) Vegetable Stock (see page 156)

1 tablespoon mild garam masala paste

sea salt

Steam the cauliflower until tender – the microwave gives very good results. Purée, stems and all, with a little cooking liquid and the stock, in a blender or food processor. When smooth, add the garam masala paste, and blend again until well amalgamated, thinning out to the desired consistency with more stock if necessary. Heat through, and season with a little sea salt. Serve hot.

You can garnish each bowl of soup with some tiny pieces of raw cauliflower, or sprinkle with roasted flaked almonds, if you wish.

Cauliflower SALADS

Raw cauliflower florets are an excellent basis for many delicious salads. Here are a few suggestions:

• with chopped hazelnuts, in Vinaigrette (see page 155) made with hazelnut or walnut oil

• raw florets alone, in a dressing of yoghurt mixed with *Moutarde de Meaux*, or Aioli (see page 154)

• with crisp mangetout and waxy potatoes, in Mayonnaise (see page 122) flavoured with a little curry powder or paste

Cauliflower Noisette

Nut butter, or beurre noisette, *is made by simply heating butter or margarine until it is so hot that it turns nut-brown and has, indeed, a nutty taste. It has a special affinity with cauliflower, one of the finest vegetables on the patch. You can make this with or without cheese.*

SERVES 4–6

1 large cauliflower, broken into florets

salt

75 g (3 oz) margarine or butter

50 g (2 oz) Gruyère cheese, finely grated

flaked almonds, toasted, to garnish

Cook the cauliflower in boiling salted water, so that it still has 'bite'. Drain well. Heat the butter or margarine in a thick pan until it turns a light hazelnut colour.

Put the cauliflower into a buttered heatproof dish, and sprinkle with the finely grated Gruyère. Heat through under the grill and, just before serving, spoon the warm *beurre noisette* over the top.

Aubergines

This exotic-looking fruit is a member of the nightshade family and probably originated in India. Aubergines range through purple to whitish-cream in colour, and grow in tropical and subtropical zones all the year round. They were adopted by the British when the Indians – who call them 'brinjal' – introduced them to their rulers under the Raj. They are also known as 'egg-plant' because of their shape.

Aubergines with Pasta and Cheese

If you are successful at growing your own aubergines under glass, the traditional ways to cook them are in moussaka, or fried in olive oil, or as fritters. But, to beat them all, try this recipe.

SERVES 4

2 medium aubergines

salt and freshly ground black pepper

olive oil for frying

300 ml (½ pint) Fresh Tomato Sauce (see page 102)

225 g (8 oz) pasta shapes, such as twists, shells or

quills, cooked *al dente*

225 g (8 oz) Cheddar or Pecorino cheese, finely

grated

1–2 cloves garlic, peeled and crushed

Cut the aubergines into thin slices, and sprinkle with salt. Leave to sweat for 30 minutes, then wipe dry. Cook the slices gently in olive oil until soft and lightly browned on both sides – they will absorb a lot of oil so keep the pan replenished.

Butter an ovenproof dish, and cover the bottom with a thin layer of Fresh Tomato Sauce. Cover with a layer of the aubergine, then a layer of pasta, then a layer of grated cheese, seasoning with garlic, salt and pepper as you go. Continue layering until all the ingredients are used up, finishing with a layer of the cheese. Bake in a preheated oven at 180°C/350°F/mark 4 for 25 minutes. Serve immediately.

Tomatoes The tomato is a native of Mexico, and its name comes from

their *tomatl*. In spite of being related to the deadly nightshade and thought at first to be poisonous, the tomato survived rural superstition to become one of our most popular vegetables.

Summer Tomato Soup *When your tomato crop is at its height in summer, this soup is a wonderful way of using it – and it also freezes extremely well.*

SERVES 6

1 onion, peeled and finely chopped	1 tablespoon tomato purée
700 g (1½ lb) tomatoes, coarsely chopped	a few thin strips of orange rind
2 cloves garlic, peeled and finely chopped	1 small bayleaf
25 g (1 oz) butter or margarine	2 tablespoons chopped fresh parsley
900 ml (1½ pints) Vegetable Stock (see page 154)	salt and freshly ground black pepper
	1 tablespoon chopped fresh tarragon, to garnish

Cook the chopped onions, tomatoes and garlic very gently in the butter or margarine in a covered pan, stirring occasionally, for about 20 minutes, until very soft. Purée in a blender or food processor.

Return to the pan with the stock, tomato purée, strips of orange rind, bayleaf and parsley. Bring to the boil, then season to taste. Simmer very gently for 10 minutes, then remove the bayleaf. Serve hot or chilled. Just before serving, stir in the chopped tarragon.

Tomato Tart
The first tomatoes were yellow, and were widely known as the 'golden apple' (thought to be a dangerous love potion with special magic). The Italian for tomato still reflects this – pomodoro is a literal translation. It was the Italians who invented the ultimate tomato tart, the pizza, but here is an old English version which makes a welcome change.

SERVES 4–6

1 recipe quantity Shortcrust Pastry (see page 150)

700 g (1½ lb) tomatoes, sliced

salt and freshly ground black pepper

75 g (3 oz) fine oatmeal

olive oil for frying

a large bunch fresh basil, chopped

3 tablespoons grated Cheddar cheese

Roll out the pastry, and use to line a 22 cm (9 in) tart tin. Season the tomato slices with salt and pepper. Dip in the oatmeal until well coated, then fry them in olive oil until the oatmeal forms a golden crust. Pile into the pastry case, making layers with the basil. Sprinkle the cheese over the top, and bake in a preheated oven at 220°C/425°F/mark 7 for 15 minutes, then at 190°C/375°F/mark 5 for a further 2 minutes. Cool a little on a wire rack before serving.

Fresh Tomato Sauce
Tomato sauce has long been popular in English food, both rural and urban: 'Chops and Tomato Sauce. Yours, Pickwick,' writes Charles Dickens in the Pickwick Papers *(1836), and what has changed? Making this sauce with your own sun-ripened tomatoes is the best of all, so make lots when your annual crop is at its height, and freeze it for use throughout the year.*

MAKES 900 ML (1½ PINTS)

450 g (1 lb) very ripe tomatoes, skinned (see below)

medium bunch fresh mixed herbs, such as parsley,
  tarragon, savory, thyme, chervil, sage, etc.

4 spring onions, trimmed and sliced

450 ml (¾ pint) canned tomato juice, or Vegetable
  Stock (see page 154), or a mixture of both

salt and freshly ground black pepper

Remove the woody parts from the centres of the tomatoes, and chop the flesh coarsely. Put into a blender or food processor with the herbs and spring onions. Whizz to a purée. Add the tomato juice and/or stock, and heat through very gently for 10 minutes. Season to taste with salt and pepper.

TO SKIN TOMATOES: Cover with boiling water, and leave for 2–3 minutes. Then pierce with a sharp knife, and the skin will peel off easily.

Right: *Fresh tomato sauce*

*B*road Beans

Broad beans are one of mankind's oldest cultivated vegetables, and are especially renowned for their affinity with bacon. In the words of G. K. Chesterton, in *The Englishman*, 1902:

But since he stood for England

And knew what England means,

Unless you give him bacon

You must not give him beans.

Broad beans are exquisite eaten young, cooked with a sprig of parsley which brings out their flavour, just as a sprig of mint enhances peas. Serve them hot, buttered or with a little cream, or cold in salads during the early summer.

Broad Bean and Mushroom Salad
The contrasting flavours and textures of broad beans and mushrooms make this a particularly memorable salad.

SERVES 3–4

225 g (8 oz) small, shelled broad beans, cooked

175 g (6 oz) button mushrooms, wiped and thinly sliced

1–2 teaspoons garam masala powder

1–2 tablespoons Vinaigrette (see page 155)

small bunch fresh coriander, finely chopped

Mix together the cooked broad beans and the sliced mushrooms in a serving bowl. Mix garam masala powder to taste into the Vinaigrette. Pour over the vegetables, toss all together with the chopped coriander, and serve slightly chilled.

Broad Bean Soup
The strong, earthy flavour of broad beans is wonderful in soup, especially made with the young, whole pods and served with a sprinkling of summer herbs. Serve with warm wholemeal bread.

SERVES 4–6

900 g (2 lb) small young broad beans, whole, topped and tailed

2 spring onions, trimmed

a handful of outer lettuce leaves, washed and torn

1.2 litres (2 pints) Vegetable Stock (see page 154)

300 ml (½ pint) milk

3 tablespoons cream

chopped fresh summer savory or mint, to garnish

Put the broad beans, spring onions and torn lettuce leaves into a big pan. Cover with the stock, and simmer until tender, about 12–15 minutes. Strain, reserving the liquid. Put the beans into a blender or food processor with enough of the liquid to blend to a smooth, thick soup. Add the milk, reheat and then stir in the cream. Sprinkle with chopped summer savory or mint just before serving.

Mangetout

You eat mangetout whole, hence their name. They are good, both lightly cooked and raw, in salads, especially mixed with ripe avocado. Sometimes they are referred to as 'snow peas' or 'sugar peas'.

Stir-Fried Mangetout

Mangetout are delicious stir-fried, retaining all their crispness, flavour and colour. You can put them into a mixed stir-fry of summer vegetables, or simply cook them on their own as here, with ginger, garlic and black bean sauce.

SERVES 3–4

3 tablespoons groundnut oil

450 g (1 lb) mangetout, topped and tailed

2 tablespoons soy sauce

1 cm (½ in) root ginger, peeled and finely grated

1 medium clove garlic, peeled and crushed

1–2 teaspoons black bean sauce to taste

3 tablespoons dark sesame oil

Heat the groundnut oil in a wok or large frying pan, and toss in the mangetout. Stir-fry over a high heat until heated through but still crisp. Turn the heat down, add the soy sauce, and cover the pan. Cook gently for a few minutes, until the mangetout soften a little. Meanwhile, combine the grated ginger, crushed garlic, black bean sauce and dark sesame oil. Stir this mixture into the mangetout, cook for a further minute or so to heat through, and then serve.

Runner Beans

The only way to eat these delectable beans is young, fresh from the vine, shredded or finely sliced (diagonally), then boiled or steamed until just tender and served with a knob of butter. Wonderful! On the whole they don't respond to the alchemy of *haute cuisine*, so keep them simple.

Sweetcorn

Sweetcorn was first grown as a crop in Mexico as far back as 7000 BC, and the South Americans still grow many varieties, including a purple Peruvian corn. It was the principal food of the Aztec, Mayan and Inca Indians of South America, and it was they who first discovered popcorn!

Sweetcorn Fines Herbes

Ears of sweetcorn are always best straight from the vine, freshly picked and simply plunged into boiling water. Traditionally served just with melted butter, this addition of fresh herbs is a delectable improvement.

SERVES 4

4 sweetcorn cobs

75 g (3 oz) butter or margarine

4 tablespoons finely chopped mixed fresh herbs, such as basil, dill, thyme, coriander, marjoram, mint, chives, etc., or 2 tablespoons dried herbs

sea salt

Trim the corn cobs, removing stem and husks and all the hairy fibres. Spread with softened butter or margarine, and roll in very finely chopped fresh herbs of your choice. Sprinkle with a little sea salt. Wrap in foil, and bake in a preheated oven at 180°C/350°F/mark 4 for 15 minutes. Serve in the foil packet, rolling in the buttery herby juices before you take each bite.

Corn à la Crème

A simple dish of sweetcorn mixed with herbs and crème fraîche *makes a delicious side vegetable. To make a more substantial dish, you can lay the creamed corn on a bed of rice, and bake it in the same way. It is wonderful, and a complete meal in itself with a tossed mixed salad.*

SERVES 4

4 corn cobs, or 450 g (1 lb) canned sweetcorn, drained

150 ml (¼ pint) *crème fraîche*

150 ml (¼ pint) single cream

salt and freshly ground black pepper

25 g (1 oz) butter or margarine

Scrape the corn off the cobs if using fresh, or use canned corn, and mix into the *crème fraîche* and single cream. Season to taste. Rub a gratin dish with the butter or margarine, and put the corn mixture in it. Bake in a preheated oven at 170°C/325°F/mark 3 for 35–45 minutes, until the top is golden. Serve immediately.

Baby Sweetcorn with Coriander
This dish of baby cobs is out of this world, truly epicurean, and I have had many a demand for the recipe. It goes beautifully as a side dish to accompany the Asparagus Tart on page 85.

SERVES 4

5 tablespoons olive oil

450 g (1 lb) baby sweetcorn

4–5 spring onions, trimmed and finely chopped

small bunch fresh coriander, finely chopped

2 cloves garlic, peeled and crushed

2.5 cm (1 in) root ginger, peeled and grated

300 ml (½ pint) *crème fraîche*

sprigs of fresh coriander, to garnish

Heat half the oil in a large pan, and gently turn the baby sweetcorn in it for 6–7 minutes, stirring all the time. Cover with a lid and leave to steam for 5 minutes. Remove the corn from the pan when it begins to soften. Add more oil to the pan, stir in the spring onions, and sauté gently until soft, about 5 minutes. Add the chopped coriander, garlic and ginger, and stir-fry for a further 2 minutes. Return the baby sweetcorn to the pan, and cook gently, covered, stirring from time to time, for a further 10 minutes. Remove from the heat, and allow to cool for 5 minutes. Then stir in the *crème fraîche*. Serve warm or cold, garnished with sprigs of coriander.

Green Beans
The French bean, a tender annual variety of the green bean genus, probably originated in South America but has long been cultivated in many other tropical, subtropical and temperate areas of the world. Green beans were brought back to Europe by the conquering Spanish, and cultivated specially by the French, hence the name of one of the finest species. There are many varieties of green bean, two of which mature to provide the kidney and haricot beans. French beans are closely related to the Scarlet Runner Bean.

Green Beans à la Francaise
This is how Eliza Acton cooked green beans in the nineteenth century, and very good it is too: a simple, lemony fresh side dish with a classic feel to it. It is delicious with grilled fish and a tossed salad.

SERVES 4

700 g (1½ lb) green beans, topped and tailed

25 g (1 oz) butter or margarine

1 tablespoon flour

salt and freshly ground black pepper

150 ml (¼ pint) Vegetable Stock (see page 154)

2 egg yolks

1 tablespoon lemon juice

Simmer the beans until tender, about 8 minutes, and then drain them. In a fresh pan, melt the butter or margarine, and stir in the flour until smooth. When lightly browned, season with salt and pepper, and gradually pour in the stock, stirring until smooth. Add the beans and toss. Off the heat, stir in the egg yolks and lemon juice, and serve at once.

Green Bean and Cauliflower Salad
As a summer salad this is hard to improve upon. The touch of mint and garlic in the dressing of good olive oil and lemon juice gives extra zest to the fresh, crisp vegetables. Serve it as a starter, with fresh wholemeal bread, or as part of a buffet table.

SERVES 4–6

1 small cauliflower, divided into florets

225 g (8 oz) green beans, topped and tailed

2 tablespoons finely chopped fresh mint

1-2 cloves garlic, peeled and crushed

5 tablespoons olive oil

1-2 tablespoons lemon juice

sea salt

Simmer the cauliflower and beans separately, until tender but still slightly crisp. Drain well, and arrange in a shallow dish. Sprinkle with the chopped mint. Add the crushed garlic to the olive oil, and mix in lemon juice and sea salt to taste. Pour this dressing evenly over the vegetables, and leave in a cool place for 30 minutes to 1 hour before serving. Do not chill.

Peas Tiny young peas,

fresh from the garden and cooked with mint, are deservedly popular side vegetables. Try the following recipes, too.

Q: How do you boil peas?

A: Briskly, ma'am.

Finchley Manual for the Training of Servants, 1800

Risi e Bisi *A simple dish of Italian inspiration, this makes a satisfying meal served with a tossed salad.*

SERVES 4–6

40 g (1½ oz) butter or margarine

1 small onion, finely chopped

325 g (12 oz) shelled garden peas

900 ml (1½ pints) Vegetable Stock (see page 154)

175 g (6 oz) basmati rice

1 teaspoon dried oregano

grated Parmesan cheese, to serve

Melt the butter or margarine, and cook the onion very gently, covered, for about 10 minutes, stirring from time to time, until soft. Stir in the peas, and when covered with the fat, pour in half of the stock. When it is bubbling add the rice, the rest of the stock and the oregano. Cook gently, covered with a lid, for about 10 minutes. Check that it does not dry out, adding more stock if necessary. Stir as little as possible, otherwise the peas will break up. When the rice is cooked, serve, passing a bowl of grated Parmesan cheese around.

Green Pea Soup 'St Germain' *The bright, deep green colour of this soup is one of the delights of midsummer. Serve it hot with garlic bread, or chilled with warm pitta bread.*

SERVES 4

325 g (12 oz) shelled garden peas

1 medium potato, peeled and sliced

1 medium onion, peeled and sliced

1 medium lettuce, quartered and washed

1.2 litres (2 pints) Vegetable Stock (see page 154)

juice of ½ lemon

150 ml (¼ pint) single cream

salt and freshly ground black pepper

Put the peas, potato, onion, lettuce and half the stock into a pan, and bring to the boil. Cover, and simmer for 5 minutes. Process to a fine purée in a blender or food processor. Return to the pan with the rest of the stock, and reheat. Add the lemon juice, stir well, then stir in the cream. Season to taste and serve hot or chilled.

Right: *Risi e bisi*

Courgettes

The courgette came into English cookery in a serious way thanks to Elizabeth David: it was she who first brought it to her public in *French Provincial Cooking* in the 1960s. The courgette is an exquisite vegetable, and if you grow just three or four plants on your vegetable patch, you will be well provided for throughout the summer. You can use them raw in salads, very finely sliced, or lightly steamed as a filling for omelettes or tossed into pasta with fresh herbs and a little cream.

Courgette Soup

A delicate green starter for summer, this version of courgette soup is lightly flavoured with fresh dill, and is excellent served either hot or chilled. I like it with Melba Toast (see page 155).

SERVE 4

4 spring onions, trimmed and sliced

40 g (1½ oz) margarine

450 g (1 lb) courgettes, trimmed and thinly sliced

1 tablespoon flour

1.2 litres (2 pints) Vegetable Stock (see page 154)

salt and freshly ground black pepper

2 tablespoons chopped fresh dill

yoghurt or *crème fraîche*, to serve (optional)

Gently sauté the spring onions in the margarine for 4–5 minutes, until soft. Add the courgettes, and stir until coated. Cover, and leave for 5 minutes on a gentle heat. Sprinkle in the flour, and then gradually add half of the stock. Stir until the mixture thickens, and then simmer until the courgettes are just cooked, about 10 minutes. Purée in a blender or food processor. Return to the pan, and add the remaining stock to bring to a thin consistency. Heat through or chill, as you wish, then season to taste, and stir in the dill. Serve with a swirl of yoghurt or *crème fraîche* floating on top, if you wish.

Golden POCKETS

For a late summer dish, use the flowers of ripe courgettes to make this elegant *hors d'oeuvre*.

Stuff each courgette flower with a little stuffing (made from cooked rice or fresh breadcrumbs, chopped herbs and/or a little grated cheese, seasoning and beaten egg to bind), dip in Fritter Batter (see page 154), and deep-fry to a delicate brown. Serve garnished with baby tomatoes and sprigs of fried parsley.

Courgettes Fines Herbes
This simple, elegant way of cooking courgettes is based on a classic French recipe.

SERVES 4

700 g (1½ lb) courgettes, trimmed and
  diagonally sliced

salt

75 g (3 oz) butter or margarine, melted

175 ml (6 fl oz) *crème fraîche*

sprigs of fresh rosemary, savory, lovage, marjoram,
  fennel, etc., all finely chopped

Blanch the courgettes in boiling salted water for 3–4 minutes. Drain well, and put into a deep pan with the melted butter or margarine. Stir, cover, and leave to cook gently until tender, shaking the pan from time to time. Then, off the heat, stir in the *crème fraîche* and finally the herbs. Heat through, and serve.

Courgettes Parmigiana
A great Italian dish, this is made up of layers of courgettes, tomato sauce and cheese, baked until the top is crusty and golden brown. It makes a complete meal in itself, just served with warm granary bread and a tossed salad, full of herbs. This dish freezes well.

SERVES 6

1.5 kg (3 lb) courgettes

1 recipe quantity Fresh Tomato Sauce (see
  page 102)

225 g (8 oz) mozzarella cheese, sliced

salt and freshly ground black pepper

15 g (½ oz) Parmesan cheese, grated

olive oil

Trim and slice the courgettes 6 mm (¼ inch) thick, diagonally. Blanch in boiling water for 2–3 minutes. Drain, and arrange in layers in a deep dish with the Fresh Tomato Sauce and slices of mozzarella, seasoning each layer with plenty of salt and pepper. Repeat until all the ingredients are used up. Top with the grated Parmesan, drizzle with olive oil, and bake in a preheated oven at 180°C/375°F/mark 4 for 40–45 minutes, until the cheese is browned and crusty. Serve immediately.

Pumpkin
Cultivated since ancient times, pumpkins come in varying shapes and colours, and are a wonderful sight at the Harvest Festival.

Soup Fermière
Pumpkin soup is one of the greatest treats of early autumn, warming the first chill evenings with its golden colour and its full, rich flavour. A couple of pumpkins in the vegetable garden will go a long way to keeping you supplied with this soup, which also freezes well, so you can eat it throughout the winter months.

SERVES 6

900 g (2 lb) pumpkin, peeled, sliced and seeded

salt, freshly ground black pepper and grated nutmeg

about 150 ml (¼ pint) milk or cream

Croûtons (see page 155) and finely grated cheese, to serve

Cut the pumpkin flesh into chunks, and put into a pan with water to just cover. Add some salt and simmer, covered, for about 25–30 minutes, until the pumpkin is tender. Blend to a smooth purée with the cooking water in a blender or food processor, and thin out to the desired consistency with milk or cream. Heat through, and season to taste with pepper and nutmeg.

Serve with Croûtons and a bowl of finely grated cheese to sprinkle over the top.

Whole Baked Pumpkin
I know no better way than this of eating pumpkin: it is rich and delicious, soft and appetizing, and serves as a meal in itself with baked potatoes and a tossed salad.

SERVES 6

25 cm (10 in) diameter pumpkin

50 g (2 oz) butter or margarine

sea salt and freshly ground black pepper

450 ml (¾ pint) single cream

Cut a lid off the pumpkin at the stalk end. Scoop out the seeds and fibres. Smear the inner surface with the butter or margarine. Sprinkle sea salt and freshly ground pepper into the cavity. Replace the lid, and put into an ovenproof dish. Bake for 1 hour in a preheated oven at 190°C/375°F/mark 5, until the flesh inside is soft. Remove the lid, and pour in the cream, heated until just under boiling point. Serve the pumpkin *à la crème*, scooped straight out of the shell.

Roast Pumpkin

Pumpkin can be used in sweet dishes: spicy pumpkin pie is traditionally served at American Thanksgiving festivities. In this recipe the pumpkin is cut into small pieces and cooked like roast potatoes or parsnips: it makes a delightful change as a side vegetable for an autumnal Sunday lunch.

pumpkin, peeled, sliced and seeded	salt and freshly ground black pepper
flour, sifted	oil for cooking

Cut the slices of pumpkin into small potato-size pieces, roll lightly in sifted flour, and season with salt and pepper. Arrange in a roasting pan of hot oil, or around the Sunday joint, and baste them during the cooking time. They will take 40 minutes in a preheated oven at 190°C/375°F/mark 5.

Vegetable Marrow

This now very popular vegetable came to England at the end of the nineteenth century, so there are no old, traditional recipes for it to be found in antique cookery books. Vegetable marrows and squashes come in all shapes, sizes and colours, from the baby marrows or courgettes so well known in European cuisine, to the wide variety of summer and winter squashes that feature extensively in American cookery. You can simply bake them, or boil them, or cook them in butter with herbs, but one of the best ways to prepare them is to stuff and then bake them, wrapped in foil, which makes a wonderful autumn dish. A stuffing of tomatoes, brown breadcrumbs and parsley, bound with egg and well seasoned, is scrumptious. More substantially, you can fill the seed cavity with spicy beans and butter, or with spinach and cottage cheese, or you can make a rice stuffing with chopped onion, garlic, mint or dill, and a little cinnamon. One of my personal favourites is the buckwheat stuffing described opposite.

Autumn Stuffed Marrow *This makes a wonderful meal for those first really cold evenings of early winter, served with buttered potatoes and some grilled tomatoes.*

SERVES 4

1 teaspoon oil

175 g (6 oz) roasted buckwheat

salt and freshly ground black pepper

1 tablespoon chopped mixed fresh herbs

3 spring onions, trimmed and finely chopped

1 tablespoon margarine

2 medium carrots, peeled and grated

1 medium courgette, trimmed and grated

1 large vegetable marrow

Heat the oil in a frying pan, and quickly sauté the buckwheat over a high heat for 2–3 minutes, stirring all the time. Add 600 ml (1 pint) boiling water, cover and simmer for 15 minutes until the buckwheat is soft. Season to taste, and blend in the herbs.

Sauté the spring onions in the margarine until soft, add the grated carrots and courgette and simmer until soft. Season, and add to the buckwheat. Cut the marrow in half lengthwise, and hollow it out, removing the seeds. Fill the hollow with the buckwheat mixture, and press the two halves back together.

Wrap in foil and bake in a preheated oven at 180°C/350°F/mark 4 for 45–55 minutes, until very tender. Serve hot, cut into thick slices.

Marrow and Pineapple Jam *This translucent, golden jam is one of autumn's delights, and remains a pleasure through the gloomy days of winter. it is delectable on toast for breakfast, and equally good on fresh scones at tea time.*

MAKES 4.5 KG (10 LB)

2.7 kg (6 lb) vegetable marrow, peeled, halved and
  seeded

450 g (1 lb) canned pineapple

2.7 kg (6 lb) granulated sugar

Cut the marrow flesh into small cubes, and dice the pineapple. Put in layers with the sugar in a preserving pan, and leave overnight to extract all the juices. Boil to setting point (see page 145), pot, and seal (see page 145). Store in a cool, dark, dry place.

You can also make this jam with ginger, adding 25 g (1 oz) root ginger, bruised, to the cooking. Remove at the end of the cooking time, and then add some slices of crystallized ginger before potting.

eggs *Galore*

About Candlemas Day

Every good goose should lay

Traditional

Medieval cottagers frequently kept geese, ducks or a few hens; they were essential suppliers of eggs for the family and – principally – of poultry meat. Although the hens were not big layers as they had to scratch around for their own food, ducks and geese would provide an extra supply of rich eggs for cakes and savoury meals. Eggs were used lavishly in rich households in the old days, as their recipe books show us – full of sauces and puddings using quantities of eggs and cream which seem very unhealthy to us now. But then, in a world without modern technology, people in general led more physically active lives and could tolerate a richer diet.

There is nothing fresher or better to taste than eggs from your own hens. However, keeping them entails a job for every day of the year, so is not a hobby to be undertaken lightly. Hens have to be fed and watered daily and kept clean and disease free, and the eggs must be gathered regularly. But if you decide to have a go, you will be rewarded with a constant supply of fresh eggs, plus usually an excess for friends and neighbours.

The HENPEN OF 1615

Your henne house would be large and spacious with somewhat a high roofe and walls strong and windowes upon the sunne rising: round about the inside of the walls upon the ground would be built large pens of 3 ft high for Geese, Ducks and fowle to sit in.

Near to the eavings ... would be perches ... on which should sit your Cocks, Hennes, Capon and Turkies, each on several perches as they are disposed...

You shall gather your eggs up once a day and leave in the nest but the nest egge, and no more, and that would ever be in the afternoon when you have seene every Henne come from the nest severally. Some Hennes will by the cackling tell you when they have layd, but some will lay mute, therefore you must let your owne eye be your instruction.

Perfect Husbandry, **Gervase Markham**, *c.*1630

THE HENHOUSE

More modern instructions would decree a two-storey henhouse, large enough to allow each bird 0.25 sq m (3 sq ft), set in a run of at least half an acre, since the run soon turns to mud and can become a disease risk. Place the henhouse near a hedge or windbreak, and keep everything surrounded by wire netting for protection. The henhouse should contain nesting boxes, a litter area, and a perch on the first floor above a removable droppings board. The ground floor must be covered with soft wood shavings, straw or peat moss, about 15–20 cm (6–8 in) deep. The droppings, scraped off the boards and then dried, are rich compost material for grass, and mixed with bonfire ash make an excellent activator for the compost heap.

A food trough for wet mash needs to be large enough to allow 12–15 cm (5–6 in) access for each bird. You can fit a galvanised tube feeder for dry mash feed, one tube to every 25 birds. Modern birds need special feeds packed with protein, energy, vitamins and minerals. You can supplement this with a few household scraps, but in general these are not that nutritious and birds have small appetites. Every laying hen will eat 100–150g (4–5 oz) dry mash per day, plus a little 'scratch feed' – corn or maize scattered around the run to keep them occupied – about 25 g (1 oz) per bird per day. Some people tie outer cabbage leaves or other greens in a string bag for the birds to peck at – these not only supply vitamins and add variety, but also give a deeper colour to the yolks. Water for the drinkers should be topped up every day, allowing 300 ml (½ pint) per bird per day.

HEN MANAGEMENT

For beginners it is advisable to buy a flock at 'point-of-lay' – i.e. pullets 18–20 weeks old that have been reared from day-old chicks by specialist growers. These will have been hatched in May, so you can start your flock off in early September. Once they have settled, they should lay for 12 months without a break, your first eggs appearing in October. The best birds will continue laying in their second year, but hens are as prone to disease and predators as any other creature, so they have to be well managed. The best idea is to get a really good manual to guide you through all the pitfalls of rearing and management, broodiness and moulting and other hazards, and you should be rewarded by a good egg harvest.

If, for example, you have six birds, you should get 4–5 eggs per day. Check the nest two or three times a day (and always knock before entering – hens are nervous birds and a shock can put them off laying). Eggs store well in a cool room (under 10°C/50°F) for 3–4 weeks, pointed end down. Don't store near fish, onions or cheese, since they pick up strong smells, and don't store them in the fridge, since they deteriorate rapidly once taken out. You are allowed to sell eggs to friends and neighbours, but to sell to shops you require a licence from the Ministry of Agriculture.

Before the selective breeding of chickens, management and storage were different, and the supply of eggs seasonal, as this excerpt from Markham's *Cheap and Good Husbandry* (1613) illustrates:

If you feed your Hens often with toasts taken out of ale, or with barley boiled, they will lay soon. Now because eggs of themselves are a singular profit, you shall understand that the best way to preserve or keep them long is some think to lay them in straw, but that is too cold, and besides will make them musty; others will lay them in bran, but that will make them putrefy; and others lay them in salt, but that makes them diminish. The best way then to keep them most sweet, sound and full, is only to keep them in a heap of malt, close and well covered all over.

Classic Egg Recipes
Fresh free-range eggs make all the difference to the flavour of your cooking. Eggs are so versatile, use them in omelettes, soufflés, pancakes and custards. Leftover whites from home-made mayonnaise can be used up in meringues. And nothing is easier than scrambled or poached eggs for light meals.

Vegetable Soufflés
There is a mystique about cooking soufflés that undermines the confidence of the most committed cook, but if you follow the basic instructions given below carefully, you will succeed. There are many vegetables that make sublime soufflés, for example spinach, sorrel, mushrooms, parsnips, courgettes and tomatoes.

SERVES 4–6

fresh breadcrumbs

grated Parmesan cheese

450 g (1 lb) basic vegetable, cooked, drained and
   the cooking liquid reserved

5 tablespoons Béchamel Sauce (see page 154), made
   with milk or the vegetable cooking water, or both

4 egg yolks

salt and freshly ground black pepper

fresh herbs or spices to taste

5 egg whites, very stiffly beaten

Grease a 1.5 litre (2½ pint) soufflé dish, then sprinkle the inside liberally with breadcrumbs and grated Parmesan. Chop or purée the cooked vegetables, as required. For variety you can add a few chopped mushrooms, cooked in butter with garlic, or chopped walnuts for texture. Stir in the Béchamel Sauce, and mix well, beat in the egg yolks, season, and add herbs or spices to taste. Fold in the stiffly beaten egg whites deftly and lightly, and pour into the prepared soufflé dish. Bake at 200°C/400°F/mark 6 for 25–30 minutes until well risen and golden, but still slightly runny in the centre. Get everyone sitting around the table before you take it out of the oven, and eat immediately before it sinks.

Piperade
This is an excellent lunch dish, which is quickly prepared and makes good use of both eggs and ripe tomatoes. Serve it with crusty brown bread and a tossed salad.

SERVES 3

50 g (2 oz) butter or margarine

2 medium onions, peeled and finely sliced

2 cloves garlic, peeled and finely sliced

4 large ripe tomatoes, skinned (see page 102) and
   chopped

2 canned red peppers, cut into strips

2 boiled potatoes, finely diced

6 eggs

salt and freshly ground black pepper

1 tablespoon chopped fresh parsley

Melt the butter or margarine in a heavy pan, and cook the onion and garlic in it, covered, until soft, about 10 minutes. Then turn up the heat a little, and cook until they brown lightly. Add the tomatoes, the strips of pepper and the potatoes, and cook for a further 5 minutes.

Beat the eggs lightly, and season with salt and pepper. Stir into the vegetable mixture, and continue stirring as you would for scrambled eggs, until thick and creamy but not dry. Serve immediately, sprinkled with chopped parsley.

Mayonnaise
Nothing can match home-made mayonnaise, especially if you make it with your own free-range eggs. It takes a careful hand to get it right, and patience, but it's a skill well worth acquiring .

MAKES ABOUT 450 ML (¾ PINT)

2–3 egg yolks

a pinch of salt

a pinch of dry mustard

300 ml (½ pint) olive oil

a few drops tarragon or wine vinegar

juice of about ½ lemon

Beat the egg yolks thoroughly in a small bowl, and then stir in the salt and mustard. Beating gently all the time, very gradually blend in the oil – at first add it drop by drop, then gradually increase the flow to a thin trickle. Go very slowly, stopping the oil from time to time (but continue beating) to allow the mayonnaise to thicken. Gradually increase the trickle, but don't go too fast otherwise the mayonnaise will curdle. Stir in the vinegar as the mixture thickens, to thin it out slightly. Then gradually add enough lemon juice to bring to the consistency you require. Keep in a cool place, but do not refrigerate – the eggs will degrade and the mayonnaise may separate.

Omelettes
Omelettes and quiches are perhaps the most obvious and accessible ways of using up eggs. A quiche is a quiche, but there are nuances to and variations on the omelette that are worth exploring.

YOU WILL NEED: • **eggs (2 per person)** • **oil or butter** • **salt and freshly ground black pepper** • **cream**

For preference, use a copper-bottomed saucepan for making an omelette. Smear it with a little oil or butter, and set it over a medium heat until very hot. Then pour in your omelette mixture – the requisite number of eggs (2 per person usually), beaten with salt and pepper, and a little cream if you wish. Pour into the pan, and when the mixture begins to bubble and blister, fold the lightly cooked edges towards the centre. Do this once or twice, being careful not to let the mixture overheat and dry out, or burn on the bottom. Put the filling of your choice into the centre, and flip the omelette over. Flip on to a hot plate or serving dish, and serve immediately. It should be slightly runny and creamy in the centre.

KOOKOO

A solid omelette where the egg mixture is beaten into a mixture of sautéed vegetables, then cooked gently in a covered pan for 10–15 minutes until quite set. Eat it cut into wedges, with salad and new potatoes or granary bread, or allow it to get cold and then cut into tiny squares to be served with pre-dinner drinks. It is also delicious warm. You can use potatoes, spinach, courgettes, broccoli, peas or sweetcorn for the filling, or a mixture of some of them, sautéed with softened onions if desired.

First cook the chosen vegetables gently in olive oil or butter in the pan until soft, and then pour on the omelette mixture (see above). Cover, then leave to cook over a gentle heat until the kookoo is set. Do not let the bottom burn. Then put under a grill to brown the top. Invert on to a serving dish.

Sweet SOUFFLÉ OMELETTES

A dessert variation made like a soufflé and cooked like an omelette, over a medium to gentle heat, ensuring the bottom does not brown. Eggs yolks are beaten with sugar until thick, and then the stiffly beaten whites folded in lightly. The filling – such as sugared and sliced strawberries, sweetened raspberries or slices of peach – is placed on the omelette while it is still cooking, then the omelette is flipped over the filling and cooked a little longer. If the inside is too runny to serve, put the soufflé omelette into a hot oven for 3–4 minutes, just to finish cooking. Don't put too much mixture into the pan at one time – it is best to cook these delicacies for just two people at a time. Three eggs will do four people.

Savoury Pancakes *Pancake*

Day is one of Britain's most ancient traditions to survive more or less intact into the late twentieth century. Every Shrove Tuesday races are run through certain villages, the participants tossing pancakes as they go.

But hark, I hear the Pancake Bell

The fritters make a gallant smell

Poor Robin's Almanac, 1671

MAKES 12 PANCAKES

150 g (5 oz) flour

a pinch of salt

2 large eggs

300 ml (½ pint) milk

150 ml (¼ pint) water

1 teaspoon vegetable oil

oil or fat, for cooking

a little grated cheese (optional)

Filling:

a savoury filling of your choice, such as creamed spinach, sweetcorn, mushrooms and garlic – see 'The Vegetable Patch' chapter for other ideas.

Sift the flour with the salt, and make a well in the centre. Break the eggs into the well, and mix thoroughly with a wooden spoon. Gradually add the milk and water, mixed together, and stir until completely smooth. Stir in the oil, and leave to stand in a cool place for 2 hours.

To cook, lightly grease a heavy-bottomed frying pan, and heat it through until pretty hot but not quite smoking. Pour 1–2 tablespoons of the batter into the pan. Immediately swirl the pan so that the batter covers the bottom evenly, and cook over a medium heat until the batter is set and lightly browned. Loosen the edges and then flip the pancake over to cook the other side. Continue until all the batter is used up, stacking the pancakes on top of each other as you take them out of the pan and keeping them warm.

Roll up some of the chosen filling inside each pancake. Place the pancakes side by side in an ovenproof dish, sprinkle with grated cheese, if desired, and bake in a preheated oven at 180°C/350°F/mark 4 for 10–15 minutes, until heated through.

Sweet Pancakes
Pancakes make stylish desserts, and there are endless fillings that you can experiment with (see below). You can also vary the flavour of the pancakes themselves: add powdered ginger to the batter before cooking, or the finely grated rind of either lemon or orange. Serve the pancakes with cream or crème fraîche, *if liked.*

MAKES 10–12 PANCAKES

100 g (4 oz) plain flour

pinch of salt

25 g (1 oz) caster sugar

2 eggs

2 egg yolks

150 ml (¼ pint) single cream

150 ml (¼ pint) milk

unsalted butter for cooking

caster sugar for sprinkling

Filling:

a sweet filling of your choice, such as home-made
    jam, soft summer fruits, stewed fruit, etc. – see
    below for suggestions.

Sift the flour and salt together, and stir in the sugar. Make a well in the centre of the mixture, and put the eggs and egg yolks into the well. Gradually mix in the flour, and beat until smooth. Add the cream and milk gradually until you have a smooth batter. Leave to stand in a cool place for at least 1 hour.

Use 1 tablespoon of the mixture to make each pancake, cooking them in unsalted butter as for the Savoury Pancakes, opposite.

Spread each warm pancake with some of the chosen sweet filling, and then roll up. Sprinkle lightly with caster sugar, and serve.

SUGGESTED SWEET PANCAKE FILLINGS: The following recipes make ideal fillings for pancakes:

- Quince Cream (see page 20)
- Cotignac (see page 20)
- Damson Cheese (see page 25)
- Apricot Fool (see page 32)
- Hunza Jam (see page 32)
- Eighteenth-Century Apricot Ice Cream (see page 33)
- Strawberries in Cream (see page 38)
- Strawberry Sauce (see page 38)
- Seventeeth-Century Raspberry Cream (see page 40)
- Blackcurrant Jelly (see page 43)
- Gooseberry Fool (see page 47)
- Gooseberry and Elderflower Compote (see page 47)

Classic Egg Desserts There are so many

ways of using eggs in puddings that it is difficult to be selective. Meringue baskets filled with fresh fruit make wonderful summer desserts, as do the many variations on the theme of custard-based puddings.

A Caramel Custard *This recipe is for a good old-fashioned* crème caramel.

SERVES 4

3 tablespoons granulated sugar

2 tablespoons water

600 ml (1 pint) milk

1 vanilla pod

2 eggs

50 g (2 oz) caster sugar

Take an ordinary cake tin, and sprinkle in the granulated sugar over the bottom. Moisten with the water, and set on a heated ring over a low heat until the sugar dissolves. Then turn the heat up, and boil briskly to a thick caramel colour, tilting the tin around and around so that the caramel cooks evenly. Remove from the heat, and leave to cool and set.

Simmer the milk with the vanilla pod for 5 minutes, then cool a little. Beat the eggs with the caster sugar until thick, then pour on the warm milk, beating all the time. Pour on to the set caramel in the tin. Bake in a preheated oven at 150°C/300°F/mark 2 for 1–1½ hours, until it has set thoroughly. Cool completely in the tin before turning out on to a serving dish – the brown top will be glossy and the caramel sauce will run down the sides. Chill before serving.

Îles Flottantes *A very light dessert, 'floating islands' are a masterpiece of French cuisine, and one of my favourite desserts. The pure white froth of the 'islands', floating in a 'sea' of pale yellow custard, are as much a pleasure to the eye as they are to the palate.*

SERVES 4

4 egg whites

a pinch of salt

100 g (4 oz) caster sugar

2 recipe quantities *Crème Anglaise* (see page 153)

flaked almonds, toasted

Fill a shallow pan with water, and bring to simmering point. Beat the egg whites with a pinch of salt until they form stiff peaks. Whisk in the caster sugar gradually until the mixture becomes smooth and shiny. Spoon 4 tablespoon-sized heaps separately into the simmering water, and poach these 'islands', turning once, for about 2–3 minutes, until risen and lightly set. Remove with a slotted spoon, and drain on a rack. Dry on absorbent kitchen paper, and place in a 'lake' of *Crème Anglaise*. Chill thoroughly. Just before serving, sprinkle with the toasted almonds.

Queen of Puddings *This old-fashioned pudding is not just a useful way of using up eggs, it has become a classic for good reason. Wonderful for all seasons, it is sweet and comforting.*

SERVES 4

75 g (3 oz) fresh breadcrumbs

600 ml (1 pint) milk

25 g (1 oz) butter or margarine

grated rind of ½ lemon

3 eggs, separated

175 g (6 oz) caster sugar

3 tablespoons raspberry jam

glacé cherries, to decorate

Grease a 1 litre (1¾ pint) ovenproof dish, and sprinkle the breadcrumbs over the bottom. Bring the milk to a slow simmer with the butter or margarine and all but 1 teaspoon of the lemon rind, then leave to cool. Beat the egg yolks with half of the caster sugar. Strain the milk on to the beaten egg yolks, and stir until the mixture is quite smooth. Pour over the breadcrumbs and leave to soak for 15 minutes.

Stand the dish in a tin of hot water, and bake in a preheated oven at 180°C/350°F/mark 4 for 25–30 minutes, until lightly set in the centre. Cool a little on a wire rack. Warm the jam, and trickle it over the top of the pudding. Finally, beat the egg whites until very stiff, and gradually whisk in the remaining 75 g (3 oz) caster sugar. Beat until stiff and glossy. Fold in the remaining lemon rind, and pile the meringue on top of the pudding. Return to the oven, at the same temperature, for a further 20 minutes, until the meringue is crisp and lightly browned. Cool on a rack, decorate with glacé cherries, and serve warm or cold.

In summer serve this with a bowl of fresh raspberries. You could also use lemon curd in place of the raspberry jam.

Crème aux Fraises *For using up extra egg whites – for example, after making Mayonnaise (see page 122) or Crème Anglaise (see page 153) – this delicate dessert is beyond compare. Simplicity itself, it retains the freshness of ripe strawberries, is light in texture, and the most beautiful of summery pinks.*

SERVES 4

450 g (1 lb) strawberries, washed, dried and hulled

2–3 tablespoons caster sugar

300 ml (½ pint) double cream, whipped

2 egg whites, stiffly beaten

Reserving four strawberries for garnish, purée the rest in a blender or food processor, and sweeten with the sugar. Stir into the whipped cream. Then carefully fold in the very stiffly beaten egg whites. Spoon into individual glass dishes, and chill. Decorate with the reserved strawberries, halved, just before serving.

Custard Tart *A light egg custard set inside a sweet pastry crust is traditional country fare. Made well, so that the custard is lightly set and not too sweet, it is delectable.*

SERVES 4

1 recipe quantity Sweet Crust Pastry (see page 150)

300 ml (½ pint) single cream or milk

1 vanilla pod

strip of lemon peel

2 eggs and 1 egg yolk

75 g (3 oz) caster sugar

grated nutmeg

Roll out the pastry, and use to line a 20 cm (8 in) tart tin. Heat the cream or milk in a heavy saucepan with the vanilla pod and lemon peel, and bring slowly to simmering point. Leave to infuse for 10 minutes. Bring to the boil again, and remove from the heat. Cool. Beat the eggs, egg yolk and sugar together until pale and thick. Strain the warm milk on to the egg mixture, stirring all the time, and then pour carefully into the prepared pastry case. Sprinkle with grated nutmeg.

Bake in a preheated oven at 170°C/325°F/mark 3 for 30–40 minutes, until the top is firm to the touch. Remove from the heat, and cool on a wire rack. Eat when cold – best eaten the same day.

Left: *Crème aux fraises*

field and *Hedgerow*

These hedgerows, hardly hedgerows,

little lines of sportive wood run wild.

William Wordsworth (1770–1850)

Food from the hedgerows has been aptly named 'food for free'. Well over a hundred wild plants are, strictly speaking, edible, but here I am focusing on those which I regard as particularly delicious – indeed essential to my personal enjoyment of the seasons. Many of them are so prolific that there is no risk of their being obliterated: nettles, blackberries, elder and fat hen, for example, have survived picking for centuries, and many a gardener respects their persistence. Yet these 'weeds', as we derogatively term them, have greater virtues. They have lovely tastes, and many are highly nutritious. The wild fruits of the autumn hedgerows are well known for their flavours, and some are even grown commercially because they are so popular.

One of the best things about hedgerow cookery is that it is fun. You go for a walk along a country lane, basket in hand and come back with a sense of pleasurable excitement in your 'finds'. What can match the feeling of the first days of spring, with their indescribable freshness, and a walk by the fields, collecting young nettle tops for soup? Or picking elderflowers in a meadow in summer? Or blackberrying in the first mists of autumn, as the leaves begin to turn red-gold, and scarlet rosehips hang in the quiet hedgerows? This experience of the seasons is, in my opinion, considerably more delightful than a trip to the local supermarket.

Also, hedgerow cookery is part of an extremely ancient tradition. Throughout history man ate what was around him, and was far more familiar then we are today with the plants that had so much to offer him in his life. From eating what grew and lived around him, man moved on to farm and cultivate, losing sight of his original food source. It is only very recently that we in the West have bought our food with money, making us slaves to whatever is offered on the shop shelf. Old cookery books abound with recipes for wild plants, as naturally they do for fish or game. And not without good reason – everyone has heard of nettle soup simply because it is delicious. There is a hidden harvest out there which is ours for the picking – judiciously, of course, and always observing the countryside code.

Remember it is illegal to pick protected plants, and you should always pick your plants sparingly rather than denuding one area. Watch your step as you go, and don't trample delicate plants under your feet. Don't

pick from roadsides, since the plants will be contaminated by exhaust fumes, and do not trespass on private land. Observing these courtesies, we can enjoy the abundance of the countryside through its changing seasons, filling our baskets with natural produce which will reward us with its wonderful flavours.

The selection of recipes that follows will help you make the most of your 'finds', and open up a whole new culinary experience.

A FEAST OF MUSHROOMS

From earliest times man has learned by trial and error the epicurean delights of wild mushrooms, and it is hard to match the excitement and pleasure of a trip into the woods and fields on a mushroom hunt. But even now, after centuries of study, there is still no theoretical way of distinguishing the edible from the poisonous – you can only tell by eating them, occasionally with fatal results. So man has cultivated a completely safe mushroom, *Agaricus bisporus*, which is what 'mushroom' means to most of us: the one we buy in the supermarkets.

But there are estimated to be over 2,000 species of edible fungi in the world (let alone inedible and invisible ones). In Britain, for example, there are around 200 which are edible, many of them in the realms of gastronomy. There are certain ones which are easily identifiable, and well worth taking home in your basket: beefsteak fungi, blewits, boletis, chanterelles, fairy-ring mushrooms, field mushrooms, honey fungi, horse mushrooms, horn of plenty, milk caps, mores, parasol mushrooms, puffballs, oyster mushrooms, shiitake mushrooms, shaggy ink caps, and wood hedgehogs. My best advice is that you consult a good mushroom guide in order to identify your finds. And if in doubt, don't eat them!

The mystery of the mushroom is that it is neither plant nor animal: it belongs to the world of microbes. By definition, mushrooms represent the group of fungi which form fruiting bodies visible to the naked eye, rather than microscopic ones. 'Toadstool' is the traditional term for a poisonous fungus, but it is a vague and unsafe differentiation, since the margin between delicious mushroom and poisonous toadstool is narrow.

Mushrooms grow almost anywhere where there is dead organic matter: compost, leaf litter, topsoil, straw or dead wood. They are part of a vital ecological cycle in which plants produce, animals consume, and fungi reduce again. They play an essential part in the decomposition process, breaking down matter which can then be re-utilized. Mushrooms can be found almost all the year round. Spring is the season of cap and bracket fungi: St George's mushroom appears in April, as do morels. Summer sees the fairy-ring mushroom, boleti and the edible field and horse mushrooms. Russulas are at their prime towards the end of the summer, and in the early autumn there is often a vast crop of mushrooms in both field and woodland.

Mushrooms are ephemeral: they appear, mature and vanish in the space of a few days, perhaps weeks, and seldom appear twice in the same place. But if you keep your eyes open as you walk the fields and woods, you may be rewarded with a wonderful dinner.

Deep-Fried Mushrooms

Before people understood the nature of spore dispersal in mushrooms, they attributed fairy rings to fantastic phenomena: either it was where lightning struck the ground, or it was snails moving around in perfect circles, or it was fairies catching colts grazing in the fields and riding around on their backs, or even the Devil beating out a track during his nocturnal prowlings. Whichever, if you are lucky enough to come across a fairy ring of mushrooms they make marvellous eating.

small field mushrooms, or any edible wild
  mushrooms, wiped and sliced

Fritter Batter (see page 154)
oil for deep-frying

Dip each mushroom, or slice of mushroom, into the batter until coated all over.

Heat the oil to a very high temperature, then deep-fry the mushrooms for about 1 minute, turning until golden all over. Drain on absorbent kitchen paper, and serve immediately.

Try the mushrooms dipped into spiced yoghurt, or into soy sauce mixed with grated root ginger and a little garlic – both are tasty accompaniments.

Potted MUSHROOMS

When the moon is at the full,
Mushrooms you may freely pull;
But when the moon is on the wane,
Wait till you think to pluck again.

This old Essex saying may have been familiar to Eliza Acton when she wrote her cookery book in 1845. Here is her way of preserving the rich harvest of mushrooms to eat throughout the lean days of winter.

Prepare either small flaps or buttons with great nicety, without wetting them, and wipe the former very dry, after the application of the salt and flannel. Stew them quite tender, with the same proportion of butter as the mushrooms au beurre [40 g (1½ oz) to 600 ml (1 pint)], and salt, cayenne and ground mace; when they are done turn them into a large dish, spread them over one end of it, and raise it two or three inches that they may be well drained from the butter. As soon as they are quite cold, press them very closely into small potting pans; pour lukewarm clarified butter thickly over them, and store them in a cool dry place. If intended for present use, merely turn them down upon a clean shelf; but for longer keeping cover the tops first with very dry paper, and then with melted mutton-suet. We have ourselves had the mushrooms, after being simply spread upon a dish while hot, remain perfectly good in that state for seven or eight weeks; they were prepared late in the season, and the weather was consequently cool during the interval.

Mushrooms in Garlic Butter

In some parts of Europe there exists a tale that when St Peter was walking through a forest with Christ, eating bread that some villagers had given them, he spat some out on the ground and this turned into mushrooms. The Devil, who was close behind, also spat on the ground and up sprang brightly coloured, poisonous toadstools. Other folklore claims that manna was mushrooms, which also seem to appear miraculously.

SERVES 3–4

450 g (1 lb) wild mushrooms, such as puffballs, field mushrooms, ceps, chanterelles or boleti

75 g (3 oz) butter or margarine

2–3 cloves garlic, peeled and crushed

sea salt and freshly ground black pepper

chopped fresh parsley, to garnish

Clean and dry the mushrooms, and trim off any shaggy parts. Slice evenly.

Heat the butter or margarine in a large, heavy pan, and toss the sliced mushrooms in it until they are well coated, and beginning to soften and cook through. Then add the crushed garlic, and cook for a further 1–2 minutes, tossing frequently. Remove from the heat, and season to taste with sea salt and pepper. Toss again, leave for several minutes in the pan, covered, for the juices to run, and then serve on hot plates, sprinkled with chopped fresh parsley.

Hops à l'Anvernoise

The French are very fond of hop tops – 'jets d'houblon' – and make a wonderful soup with them. This simple way of cooking them as a side vegetable is exquisite, too – well worth a try if you live where wild hops are plentiful.

YOU WILL NEED: • hop tops, washed • Vegetable Stock (see page 154) • butter or margarine • cream • salt and freshly ground black pepper

Boil the hop tops – the top four leaves – in stock until tender, about 5–6 minutes. Drain, then toss over a low heat with a little butter or margarine until well coated. Add a little cream to the pan, mix well, and season to taste. Serve immediately.

Comfrey Pie
Comfrey contains all the goodness of spinach, plus the valuable Vitamin B12, which is otherwise not found in the vegetable world. It has a higher protein content than any other vegetable except the soya bean, and has been eaten by man for over a thousand years. It also has great healing powers, and is known in herbal medicine for its ability to help hasten the mending of fractured bones. A really delicious vegetable, too, as this pie demonstrates.

SERVES 4

1 recipe quantity Oil Pastry (see page 152)

325 g (12 oz) comfrey, washed, drained, chopped, and lightly cooked

2 cloves garlic, peeled and crushed

1 recipe quantity Béchamel Sauce (see page 154)

salt and freshly ground black pepper

2 tablespoons double cream

2 eggs, separated

Press the pastry, with your knuckles, into a greased 22 cm (9 in) pie dish. Bake blind (see page 152) in a pre-heated oven at 170°C/325°F/mark 3 for 10–15 minutes, until set and lightly golden.

Mix the comfrey and crushed garlic into the Béchamel Sauce, season to taste, and add the cream. Add the egg yolks to the mixture. Beat the whites until stiff, and fold them in. Pour into the pastry shell, and bake in a preheated oven at 190°C/375°F/mark 5 for 25–30 minutes, until risen, golden and lightly set in the centre.

Dandelion SALADS

Dandelion gets its name from *dent de lion* meaning lion's tooth and describing its jagged leaves. Dandelion wine, made from the flowers, is a well-known country wine, but the leaves have also been used in salads for centuries. They still are in France today, tossed into mixed leaf salads and appreciated for their bitter flavour and richness of vitamins.

• Potato Salad with Dandelion: Cook waxy new potatoes, and slice them while still hot. Chop a few spring onions, crush a clove of garlic, slice some inner celery stalks very finely, and tear up some young dandelion leaves. Toss them all together with the potatoes in Vinaigrette (see page 155).

• Similarly, Beetroot and Dandelion Salad with young freshly cooked, chopped beetroot is delicious.

• Or try an Egg and Dandelion Salad: Soft-boil the eggs, and peel when they are cold. Quarter them, and place on a bed of washed, shredded dandelion leaves, dressed in Aioli (see page 154).

• Equally good is Dandelion and Pasta Salad: Just tear the young dandelion leaves into little strips, and toss with cold, cooked pasta in lots of garlicky Vinaigrette (see page 155). Add small cubes of cooked courgette, and toss again.

Nettle Soup
Young nettles are traditionally a spring tonic, made in the form of soup or tea. For country folk they were the first green vegetable to appear after a long, lean winter's diet of salted meat. They are rich in vegetable protein, minerals and vitamins, and were said to purify the blood. Pick the top six leaves when the nettles are young – with rubber gloves on! They make an inimitable soup which freezes very well.

SERVES 4

a large saucepan full of nettle tops

40 g (1½ oz) butter or margarine

25 g (1 oz) flour

900 ml (1½ pints) Vegetable Stock (see page 154)

salt and freshly ground black pepper

150 ml (¼ pint) single cream or milk

Croûtons (see page 155), to serve

Wash the nettle tops, and drain well. Cook in just the water still clinging to them, as for spinach, covered, for 10–15 minutes, until completely tender. This will neutralise the sting and release a dark coloured water. Drain well, and chop the nettles.

Melt the butter or margarine, and stir in the flour. Add the stock gradually, stirring all the time, until the mixture is smooth and thick. Simmer very gently for 5 minutes, then season to taste. Mix in the cooked nettles, and then purée in a blender or food processor. Add the cream or milk, reheat gently, and it is ready to serve. Pour into large, shallow soup dishes, and sprinkle the Croûtons over the top.

Fat Hen au Gratin
Fat hen was a common vegetable for country folk from neolithic times, superseded only when spinach – its close relative – began to be cultivated in earnest. It is a sensational vegetable, rich in the B vitamins, high in vegetable protein, and has more iron and calcium than spinach. It grows abundantly and vigorously, so you need have no fears about cropping a good harvest for yourself.

SERVES 4

700 g (1½ lb) fat hen, trimmed and washed

butter or margarine

salt and freshly ground black pepper

4 soft-boiled eggs, cooled, peeled and halved

1½ recipe quantities Béchamel Sauce (see page 154)

a little single cream

50 g (2 oz) breadcrumbs, fried in vegetable oil

Put the prepared fat hen into a large saucepan with a little water, and boil until tender, about 8 minutes. Drain and chop it, then toss in butter or margarine over a low heat, and season to taste. Cover the bottom of an oven-proof dish with the fat hen, then place the halved eggs on top. Pour the Béchamel Sauce over the top, dot with more butter or margarine, and bake in a preheated oven at 200°C/400°F/mark 6 for 20 minutes, until the top is golden. Sprinkle with the fried breadcrumbs, and serve.

Walnut Bread
The magnificent walnut tree makes a strong statement in the British landscape, with its stately growth, its large, smooth leaves and its enormous span. Its fruits, the wonderful 'wet' walnuts of the autumn, are at their best fresh. You can make soup with them, and put them into nut roasts, salads or leek dishes. This bread is also a superb way of enjoying their flavour.

MAKES 2 x 450 G (1 LB) LOAVES

2 eggs

100 g (4 oz) soft brown sugar

450 g (1 lb) plain flour

½ teaspoon salt

4 teaspoons baking powder

600 ml (1 pint) milk

175 g (6 oz) chopped walnuts

Beat the eggs well, and then beat in the brown sugar. Sift the flour with the salt and baking powder, and add alternately with the milk to the egg mixture. Stir in the chopped nuts, and pour into two greased 450 g (1 lb) loaf tins. Leave to stand, covered, in a warm place for 30 minutes. Then bake at 180°C/350°F/mark 4 for 45 minutes. Cool a little on a wire rack, and then slice and serve.

Bilberry or Blueberry cake
If you are lucky enough to live where bilberries grow plentifully in the wild – fairly northerly climes – they are a rewarding harvest. They make an excellent country wine, and a delicious pie, traditionally served for Sunday lunch with lots of thick cream! This cake, which you can also make with cultivated blueberries, is succulent, moist and very moreish. It freezes well, too, so you can enjoy it through the dark days of winter.

SERVES 8

275 g (9 oz) self-raising flour

2 teaspoons ground cinnamon

150 g (5 oz) margarine

100 g (4 oz) caster sugar

grated rind of ½ lemon

325 g (12 oz) bilberries or blueberries

2 eggs, beaten

Sift the flour with the cinnamon, and then rub in the margarine until the mixture resembles crumbs. Stir in the sugar and lemon rind, and then fold in the bilberries or blueberries carefully. Fold in the beaten eggs gently, and put into a greased 20 cm (8 in) cake tin with a removable base. Bake in a preheated oven at 180°C/350°F/mark 4 for 1¼ hours, until a knife comes out clean from the centre. Leave in the tin for about 10 minutes, then remove and place on a wire rack to cool.

Verjuice

Verjuice was in constant use until the 19th century, when its place was taken by the squeeze of lemon juice. It is really a very sharp cider – not a vinegar. The distilling was of interest, for it would account for the apparent mildness of some of the pickles made. In copying old recipes, very often a sharp cider is much nearer the original than the modern vinegar.

Food in England, Dorothy Hartley, 1954

VERJUICE OF CRAB APPLES (this was the best verjuice):'Verjuice: gather crabbs as soon as the kernels turn black, and lay they in a heap to sweat and take them into troughs and crush with beetles [heavy wooden mallet]. Make a bagge of coarse hair-cloth and fill it with the crabbes, and presse and run the liquor into Hogsheads.'

Crab Apple Jelly
Was the crab apple the tree whose fruit tempted Eve in the Garden of Eden? We may never know, but in any case the crab apple has been eaten by man since the dawn of history, and is a versatile and useful fruit. It makes the best of all the hedgerow jellies, a beautiful orange-pink colour, with an individual flavour all of its own. It is delicious with hot or cold meats, with bread and cheese, or on toast at tea time.

YOU WILL NEED: • crab apples • water • granulated sugar

Cook the crab apples with water to cover until they are very soft. Strain through a jelly bag, and leave to drip for several hours. Measure the liquid collected into a clean pan, and to every 600 ml (1 pint) liquid add 325 g (12 oz) sugar. Dissolve the sugar over a gentle heat, and then boil rapidly to setting point (see page 145). Cool a little, then pot and seal (see page 145). Store in a cool, dark place.

You can make composite hedgerow jellies *ad infinitum*. Try crab apple and blackberry, crab apple and rowanberry, crab apple and rosehip, or crab apple and elderberry. You can also add the leaf of a scented geranium to the cooking of the final jelly to add a delicate flavour. Remove it before potting the jelly.

Blackberry PURÉE

This makes a delicious fruity sauce to serve with a pudding or dessert of your choice, and makes a good base for Blackberry Ice Cream (see page 140).

Put 450 g (1 lb) blackberries, washed and hulled, into a blender or food processor with a little caster sugar, and blend to a purée. Press through a sieve to remove the pips, and sweeten to taste with more sugar. This amount will make approximately 600 ml (1 pint), according to the juiciness of the fruit.

Pickled Blackberries

The greatest taste of the hedgerow harvest, blackberries have been eaten for centuries. Other parts of the plant have been fully used too – the pliable twigs for basket work, and the leaves and roots for natural dyes. Pickling blackberries is an excellent way of preserving them, and they are wonderful with a simple lunch of bread and cheese and a salad.

MAKES 2 KG (4 LB)

450 g (1 lb) loaf sugar

300 ml (¼ pint) white vinegar

1 teaspoon allspice berries

1 teaspoon whole cloves

2 x 7.5 cm (3 in) cinnamon sticks

900 g (2 lb) blackberries, washed and hulled

Dissolve the sugar in the vinegar over a gentle heat. Put the spices in a muslin bag, add to the vinegar, and simmer for several minutes. Add the blackberries, and cook for 10–15 minutes. Remove the bag of spices, scoop out the blackberries with a slotted spoon, and pack into clean, warmed jars. Then boil the vinegar down until it turns syrupy. Pour over the blackberries in the jars to cover, and seal. Store in a cool, dark place.

Blackberry Ice Cream

This is nothing less than sublime, making the very best use of our superlative autumn hedgerow fruit. You will enjoy this as the winter days darken and the evenings close in.

SERVES 4

150 ml (¼ pint) Greek yoghurt

150 ml (¼ pint) *Crème Anglaise* (see page 153)

40 g (1½ oz) icing sugar

½ recipe quantity Blackberry Purée (see page 139)

2 egg whites

a pinch of salt

Mix the yoghurt with the *Crème Anglaise*, and sweeten with the sugar. Beat well until smooth. Fold in the Blackberry Purée. Beat the egg whites with a pinch of salt until they are very stiff, and fold into the mixture. Put into a freezer container, cover, and freeze for 1 hour, until firmish at the edge. Scoop out, and blend until smooth. Return to the container, cover and return to the freezer for the final freezing. Alternatively, use an ice-cream maker, following the manufacturer's instructions.

Right: *Pickled blackberries*

simple *Preserves*

Now it is autumn and the falling fruit

When the garden harvest provides a glut of fruits and vegetables, one of the best ways of utilizing them, apart from freezing made-up dishes, is to make preserves. Jams, jellies, chutneys, relishes and conserves

And the long journey towards oblivion

D. H. Lawrence (1885–1930)

are traditional ways of stocking the larder; there are many books devoted to the skills of good preserve-making.

Jams and Jellies

Use fruit which is firm and ripe, or just under-ripe, and of good quality. Over-ripe fruit will not produce jam which sets well. In a wet season fruit has a lower sugar content than normal, so jam or jelly made from it may not keep so well for so long. Always wash fruit before using, to remove all traces of dust and dirt. Use lump, preserving or granulated sugar – in that order of preference – and avoid the dark sugars since they change both the colour and flavour of the preserve. If you warm the sugar slightly before stirring into the fruit, it will dissolve more quickly.

CRYSTALLIZING AND PECTIN

If your jam should crystallize during storage it is due either to too much sugar, or to over-boiling. It also happens if the storage place is too dry. You can produce a short-term remedy by turning the contents of the jar into a saucepan and heating gently to near boiling point. Leave to reset in a clean jar. The jam will be satisfactory for immediate use, although it will go sugary again in time.

Pectin is a natural gum-like substance found in varying amounts in different fruits – usually in cores, pips and skin – and is essential for a good set in jams and jellies. Some fruits do not contain enough pectin for a good set, so you need to mix low- with high-pectin fruits, or add shop-bought pectin – in liquid or powder form.

Guide to PECTIN CONTENTS OF FRUIT

HIGH	MEDIUM	LOW
cooking apples	sweet apples	late blackberries
blackcurrants	fresh apricots	cherries
cranberries	early blackberries	elderberries
damsons	greengages	figs
gooseberries	peaches	guavas
grapefruit	plums	marrow
grapes	raspberries	medlars
lemons		mulberries
loganberries		pears
acid plums		rhubarb
quinces		strawberries
redcurrants		

EQUIPMENT

Preserving Pan – Choose a pan which will be large enough: it should not be more than half-full when the fruit and sugar are added, because the mixture needs to be able to boil rapidly without boiling over. Choose a heavy-bottomed aluminium or stainless-steel pan for best results. Never use an iron or zinc pan, because the acid in the fruit reacts with the metal, and both the colour and flavour of the preserve will be affected. Enamel pans do not conduct heat fast enough, and tend to burn easily. Using a copper pan destroys much of the Vitamin C content of the fruit.

OTHER EQUIPMENT

- large hair or nylon sieve (metal equipment will impair the flavour of the preserve, and can be discoloured by the acid in the fruit)
- slotted spoon
- long-handled wooden spoons
- sharp stainless-steel knives
- mincer or food processor
- serrated knife
- stoner, for stoning small fruit
- funnel
- jam thermometer
- accurate scales
- jars with plastic screw-tops (metal ones rust)
- waxed and cellophane discs
- labels

Making Jam *A jam is a conserve of fruit, boiled with sugar and water, whereas a jelly is made with the fruit juice only, boiled with sugar. A marmalade is a kind of jam made with citrus fruits. Jams must have sufficient sugar for sound storage – organisms cannot grow when the sugar content is more than 50–55 per cent. Hence the addition of lemon juice in many jam recipes – its twofold purpose being to relieve the sweetness and also to help the set. Jams are usually cooked to 104°C/220°F. Remember that it is the fruit rather than the sugar that needs cooking, so jams (and jellies) boiled for too long with the sugar tend to lose colour and flavour. Certain soft fruits can be ruined by long boiling.*

BASIC METHOD

Place washed fruit in preserving pan, with or without water as per the recipe. Cook gently, without boiling, until juices begin to run. Turn up heat, bring to boil, then simmer until tender. Add the sugar, stir over gentle heat until it dissolves. Bring to the boil, boil rapidly to setting point (see below). Pot, cover, and store (see below).

TESTING FOR A SET

Flake test – When the jam starts to thicken, dip in a wooden spoon and hold it over the pan. If, as the jam drops off the spoon, it forms a sheet and drops off as cleanly as a flake, then the jam will set when cold. If by any chance the jam fails to set, add 2 tablespoons lemon juice per 2 kg (4 lb) fruit, and try again – or add shop-bought pectin in the quantity suggested on the label.

Saucer test – When it starts to thicken, put a little jam on a cold saucer; put in a cold place. Draw jam off the heat. After 5 minutes, tilt the saucer: if the jam wrinkles a little and doesn't run, it is ready to pot. If still liquid and runs over the saucer, return jam to the heat. Continue boiling until the test is successful. The stage of boiling the sugar to setting point generally takes about 10 minutes, but depends on the water content of the fruit.

Thermometer – You will need a reliable cook's thermometer, which goes up to and includes 104°C/220°F. Always put the thermometer into hot water before use to prevent it cracking. To test for a set, stir the jam so that the temperature is even throughout, and when the thermometer reads 104°C/220°F, a good set should be obtained – although in some cases 105–6°C/221–222°F will be better.

POTTING, COVERING AND STORAGE

Let jam settle a little before potting, remove any scum with a spoon. Choose suitably sized jam jars with plastic lids: wash and rinse thoroughly in hot water, dry and keep warm in a very low oven or on top of a boiler, until ready to use. Pour or ladle jam into the jars up to the neck. Cover immediately with a waxed disc, waxed side down, to keep any dust out. Leave to cool, then place a cellophane disc over the top of each jar, and screw the plastic top down over it. Avoid metal screw-tops as they tend to corrode. Label clearly (date and contents) and store in a cool, dark, dry place. Heat will shrink the contents of the jar, light will fade it and damp will encourage mould.

Making Jellies

So long as you have the basic equipment of a jelly bag and a thermometer, making jellies is simpler than making any other preserve. Always make sure that the jelly bag is clean, by soaking it in boiling water, then wringing it out.

The most practical way of hanging a jelly bag is on the legs of an upturned chair. Tie the suspending tapes to the bars of the chair, and place a large bowl underneath to catch the drips. Never squeeze the bag to extract more juice because the jelly will turn cloudy.

BASIC METHOD

Make sure that the fruit you are using is clean and not over-ripe. Remove any stalks, but don't bother to top and tail such fruits as gooseberries and blackcurrants. Pick the fruit over and discard any that is mouldy or over-ripe. If you are gathering the fruit from the hedgerow or your own garden, it is best to pick on a dry day because fruit sodden with rain will attract mildew. Rinse the fruit to remove any dirt or grit.

Put the fruit in a preserving pan, and cook as instructed in the recipe until the fruit is soft and the juices run. Strain through the scalded jelly bag (see above), and measure the juice collected into the cleaned pan. Add the sugar – the general rule for jellies is to add 450 g (1 lb) sugar to every 600 ml (1 pint) juice. This gives a jelly which will both set and keep, although this ratio varies slightly according to the fruit.

Stir over a medium heat until the sugar dissolves, then bring to the boil and boil fast to setting point (the same as for jam – see page 145). This will take about 10 minutes, longer if the fruit has a high water content.

Skim the jelly with a metal spoon and remove the last traces of scum with a piece of absorbent kitchen paper. Pot immediately in warm, clean jars (see page 145), before it has a chance to set in the pan. Cover, and store (see page 145).

Suitable Fruits for JELLY MAKING

windfall apples	haws	raspberries
blackberries	japonica	redcurrants
blackcurrants	loganberries	rosehips
cherries	medlars	rowan
crab apples	mulberries	sloes
damsons or wild plums	pears	strawberries
elderberries	plums	white currants
gooseberries	quinces	

Chutneys A wide variety of fruits and vegetables can be used to make

chutney. Traditionally, apples and onions provided the basis, and sultanas, raisins and dates are often found in the ingredients list, too. Plums, marrows, gooseberries and tomatoes also make lovely chutney, and shallots and garlic are often added to give zest and flavour. Chutneys are frequently laced with hot spices such as chillies, peppercorns and mustard seeds to provide a hot tang.

Making Chutney *Use fresh fruit or vegetables which are not over-ripe or damaged. Prepare*

them, and put into an aluminium pan (metals such as brass, copper or iron will react with the acid in the vinegar and spoil both the chutney and the pan). Usually, unless otherwise specified in the recipe, all the other ingredients – the onions, spices, vinegar and sugar, etc. – are put in the pan together with the vegetables or fruit. They are simmered for 2–3 hours, according to the individual recipe. This long, steady cooking is required for a good chutney, but do not over-boil it. As soon as the mixture thickens to the point where pools of vinegar no longer collect on the surface, the chutney is ready.

Allow the cooked chutney to cool for a while in the preserving pan before bottling because it tends to shrink quite considerably as it loses heat. Pot in clean jam jars when tepid, prodding out any air bubbles trapped in the mixture, and making sure that the chutney is well packed down. Cover with a waxed disc, waxed side down, then put on an outer cellophane disc. Screw down with a plastic screw-top to seal – never use metal screw-tops since these tend to rust and corrode. Wipe the jars clean with a damp cloth, then label. Store in a cool, dark, dry place. Some chutneys keep for many years, and improve greatly with keeping.

Pickles and Relishes You can use a wide

range of fruits, vegetables and herbs for making pickles and relishes: cauliflower, shallots, apples, onions, artichokes, beetroot, peaches and pears, for example. Baby cucumbers and red cabbage are delicious pickled, as are mushrooms and even walnuts. The art of making good pickles is to get the right balance of sourness, saltiness and sweetness by adjusting the quantities of vinegar, salt and sugar.

Brining

Vegetables and fruits are often soaked in brine, a solution of salt and water, to help preserve them, prior to pickling in vinegar. A 10 per cent brine solution is normally used for most vegetable pickles and relishes. Sometimes vinegar is used with the brine, and then the percentage can be lowered to 5 per cent.

TO MAKE BRINE: For a 10 per cent brine solution, mix 100 g (4 oz) salt to every 1.2 litres (2 pints) water. Stir until the salt dissolves.

For a 5 per cent brine solution, mix 50 g (2 oz) salt to every 1.2 litres (2 pints) water.

BASIC METHOD FOR PICKLING

Clean and prepare the vegetables or fruit, cut up to a suitable size, and cover with a 10 per cent brine solution (see above) for 24 hours. Keep weighted down with a plate, so that the vegetables or fruit remain completely covered.

Drain, rinse thoroughly with cold water and pack into jars. Pour Spiced Vinegar (see below) over them. Cover, and seal.

Crisp pickles, such as onions and red cabbage, are best covered with cold vinegar, whereas plums, damsons and walnuts are better covered with boiling or very hot vinegar, which is allowed to cool before covering and sealing.

SPICES AND HERBS: Spices add zest and flavour to pickles and relishes, and also have the added advantage that they are preservatives in their own right. The best ones to use are cloves, cinnamon, pepper, allspice, mace, nutmeg and ginger. Ground turmeric is sometimes added for its golden colour. Herbs are a traditional addition to many relishes and pickles, notably rue, fennel, sage, coriander – and, of course, dill.

Spiced Vinegar

MAKES 1.2 LITRES (2 PINTS):

1.2 litres (2 pints) white vinegar

25 g (1 oz) root ginger

7 g (¼ oz) each whole cloves, allspice berries, cinnamon sticks and whole black peppercorns

Warm the vinegar in an aluminium preserving pan. Add the spices, cover, and infuse over a low heat for 2 hours. Leave to cool. When completely cold, strain and decant into bottles with the spices. Use as required.

basic *Recipes*

Shortcrust Pastry

FOR A 20–25 CM (8–10 IN) PASTRY CASE

225 g (8 oz) plain flour

a pinch of salt

100 g (4 oz) butter or margarine, cut into small
  pieces

Sift the flour with the salt into a large bowl. Rub in the butter or margarine until the mixture resembles fine breadcrumbs. Add a little cold water, enough to mix to a light dough. Knead on a floured surface until smooth. Chill for 30 minutes before using.

Sweet Crust Pastry

FOR A 20–25 CM (8–10 IN) PASTRY CASE

75 g (3 oz) butter or sunflower margarine, cut into
  small pieces

175 g (6 oz) plain flour, sifted

1 heaped tablespoon caster sugar

3–4 tablespoons very cold water

Rub the butter or sunflower margarine into the sifted flour until it resembles fine breadcrumbs, then mix in the caster sugar. Add the cold water, and knead the pastry on a floured surface until light and smooth. Chill for 2 hours before rolling out.

   This pastry freezes very successfully.

Oil Pastry

FOR A 20–22 CM (8–9 IN) PASTRY CASE

175 g (6 oz) plain flour

½ teaspoon salt

1 tablespoon sesame seeds (optional)

5 tablespoons vegetable oil

1½ tablespoons cold water

Sift the flour with the salt into a large bowl, and stir in the sesame seeds, if using, oil and water. Mix well, then knead briefly until smooth. Press immediately into a greased flan tin or pie dish with your knuckles. This pastry does not need chilling before use.

Blender Pastry

FOR A 20–22 CM (8–9 IN) PASTRY CASE

75 g (3 oz) soft margarine

175 g (6 oz) plain flour

3 tablespoons cold water

a large pinch salt

Put all the ingredients into a blender or food processor, and blend until they form a dough. Knead to a smooth ball, and chill for 1 hour before using.

To Bake Blind

Line the greased pie dish or tart tin with the prepared pastry. Cut out a piece of foil or greaseproof paper larger than the base of the dish or tin, and press it against the pastry. Then fill the pastry case with a 1 cm (½ in) layer of dried beans or ceramic baking beans. For a partially baked pastry case, bake in a preheated oven at 180°C/350°F/mark 4 for 10–15 minutes, then remove the foil or paper and beans, and bake for a further 5 minutes, until just firm and lightly coloured. Pastry cases which need complete baking should be returned to the oven for 15 minutes after removing the foil and beans, until firm and pale golden brown. Time and temperature may vary from recipe to recipe.

Crème Anglaise

MAKES ABOUT 600 ML (1 PINT)

75 g (3 oz) caster sugar

2 egg yolks or 1 whole egg

1 heaped teaspoon cornflour

450 ml (¾ pint) hot milk

1 teaspoon vanilla essence

Beat the sugar with the egg yolks or whole egg (the latter makes a lighter custard) until thick and creamy. The mixture will turn pale yellow. Beat in the cornflour. Continue beating while you pour on the hot milk in a thin stream, until the mixture is well blended. Pour into a heavy-bottomed saucepan and cook gently over a moderate heat, stirring all the time with a wooden spoon. When it begins to thicken and turn creamy, turn the heat down, allow it to come to a very gentle simmer, and continue stirring for 1–2 minutes. Do not let it boil hard, otherwise it will separate. Remove from the heat and stir in the vanilla essence. Leave to settle for 5–10 minutes before serving. *Crème Anglaise* can also be served cold.

Frangipani *Frangipani is an almond-flavoured* crème pâtissière *(see below), the 'pastry cream' basis of many a classic French dessert.*

1 egg

1 egg yolk

75 g (3 oz) caster sugar

50 g (2 oz) sifted flour

300 ml (½ pint) boiling milk

40 g (1½ oz) butter

2 teaspoons vanilla essence

1 teaspoon almond essence

75 g (3 oz) crushed macaroons or ground almonds,

or half and half

Beat the whole egg and egg yolk together, and gradually add the sugar, beating until the mixture is pale yellow and thick. Beat in the flour, then whisk in the hot milk in a thin stream. Pour into a heavy-bottomed saucepan, and place over a moderate heat. Stir slowly as it thickens, and when it bubbles turn the heat down and stir for a further 2–3 minutes.

Beat in the butter, vanilla and almond essences and the macaroons or almonds. Cool, and use.

Crème Pâtissière

To make, simply follow the Frangipani recipe above, omitting the almond essence and crushed macaroons or ground almonds; just flavour it with vanilla essence.

Fritter Batter

MAKES ABOUT 300 ML (½ PINT)

100 g (4 oz) plain flour

a pinch of salt

1 teaspoon baking powder

2 tablespoons olive oil

150 ml (¼ pint) warm water

1 egg white, stiffly beaten

Sift the flour with the salt and baking powder, and stir in the oil. Gradually add the water and stir well until the mixture is thick and creamy. Leave to stand for 2 hours, and then thin out with a little more water if necessary. Fold the stiffly beaten egg white into the mixture just before using it.

Vegetable Stock

If you decide not to use shop-bought stock cubes, you can easily make your own vegetable stock from vegetable trimmings.

Using the trimmings from vegetables such as onions, carrots, leeks, cabbage, tomatoes, Jerusalem artichokes, potatoes (including the peelings), cauliflower (including leaves) and so on, makes the most of them.

Simply put the trimmings into a large saucepan, and cover with cold water. Add sea salt, peppercorns and bay leaves or other herbs for flavouring, either fresh or dried and according to taste. Bring to the boil, then simmer, covered, for 1 hour. Leave to stand until cold, then strain off.

This stock will keep in the refrigerator for up to 5 days. Alternatively, it freezes very well.

Béchamel Sauce

MAKES ABOUT 400 ML (14 FL OZ)

40 g (1½ oz) butter or margarine

2 tablespoons flour

300 ml (½ pint) warmed milk

salt and freshly ground black pepper

Melt the butter or margarine in a thick-bottomed pan, and stir in the flour with a wooden spoon. Add the milk slowly, stirring all the time, until the sauce thickens. Season to taste, and simmer over a very gentle heat for 6–8 minutes. Thin out with more milk if necessary.

FOR SAUCE À LA CRÈME: Make the sauce with single cream instead of milk.

Vinaigrette

MAKES ABOUT 200 ML (7 FL OZ)

2 teaspoons Dijon mustard

2 tablespoons lemon juice or wine vinegar

sea salt and freshly ground black pepper

½ teaspoon sugar (optional)

1 clove garlic, peeled and crushed (optional)

150 ml (¼ pint) olive oil

fresh rosemary or bay leaf (optional)

Mix the Dijon mustard with the lemon juice or wine vinegar, and season with sea salt and pepper. Add the sugar and crushed garlic, if desired. Add the olive oil gradually, stirring thoroughly all the time, until the mixture thickens and amalgamates. Leave to stand for a while before using, so that the flavours blend well. Put a few rosemary leaves or a small bay leaf into the vinaigrette if you wish, and it will take on the subtle flavour of the herb.

Melba Toast

Cut the crusts off very thin slices of wholemeal, granary or white bread, according to taste. Lay them in a single layer on a baking tray, and put into a preheated oven set at 150°C/300°F/mark 2. Leave until crisp and lightly browned, about 40 minutes.

Croûtons

SERVES 4

4 slices white or brown bread, medium thick, crusts
  removed

sunflower or groundnut oil for frying

Cut the slices of bread into tiny cubes. Heat the oil gently, and fry the cubes of bread over a medium heat, shaking regularly to turn them, until they begin to crisp and eventually turn a light golden colour. Remove the croûtons from the pan with a slotted spoon, and drain on absorbent kitchen paper. Keep in a warm oven until ready to use – an ideal accompaniment to soups and salads.

menu index

index

Figures in italics refer to illustration captions.

Text copyright © Rosamond Richardson1997
Photographs copyright © Robin Matthews 1997
Design and Layout copyright © Weidenfeld & Nicolson 1997

First published in 1997 by
George Weidenfeld & Nicolson Limited
The Orion Publishing Group
Orion House
5 Upper St. Martin's Lane
London WC2H 9EA

A CIP catalogue record for this book is available from the British Library

ISBN 0-297-83258-1

Designed by Lisa Tai
Home Economist: Emma Patmore
Stylist: Roisin Nield
Typeset in Caslon, KuenstlerScript